# BURL BARER
# FRANK C. GIRARDOT JR.
# KEN EURELL

# BETRAYAL IN BLUE

## THE STORY BEHIND THE DOCUMENTARY "THE SEVEN FIVE"

WILDBLUE
PRESS

WildBluePress.com

*Some names and identifying details have been changed to protect the privacy of individuals.*

*BETRAYAL IN BLUE published by:*
*WILDBLUE PRESS*
*P.O. Box 102440*
*Denver, Colorado 80250*

*WILDBLUE PRESS is registered at the U.S. Patent and Trademark Offices.*

*ISBN 978-1-942266-74-7     Trade Paperback*
*ISBN 978-1-942266-73-0     eBook*

*Interior Formatting/Book Cover Design by Elijah Toten*
*www.totencreative.com*

"This book is dedicated to my wife, Dori. For your endless support when everything around us was falling apart. You kept the family together, your love for us never wavering. You showed strength and gave me a shoulder to lean on when it was needed most. Thank you for your never-ending love." — Ken Eurell

*Each man has been placed in a post of honor, which he must not desert. A humble workman who commits an injustice is as much to blame as a renowned tyrant. Thus we all have our choice between justice and injustice.* — 'Abdu'l-Bahá

# BETWEEN OURSELVES – OPENING COMMENTS BY BURL BARER

There is one thing upon which we all agree. None of us were brought by the stork. Planned or unplanned, we are all the product of the same process of biology and genetics. We are all influenced by what we inherit from our parents and our environment.

A child raised on a farm in the Midwest has a different perspective than one raised on the Southside of Chicago or Manhattan's Lower East Side. We can argue nature vs. nurture all day long, but it is an absolute fact that when it comes to our health and well-being, we want to know our family's medical history. It is in our best interest to know what talents, strengths, weaknesses, or illnesses exist in our DNA.

It's the same with cities.

The personality of Los Angeles is different from that of Boston; just as Boston's unique charm is distinct from that of New York City. Each town has its origin, outlook, and character, all of which are the product of its history and citizenry. All the primary characters in this story have what Billy Joel termed "A New York State of Mind."

To appreciate a rose, you do not sniff the soil from which it grew; to understand a rose, you must know the soil that nourished it and gave it life.

Described by the Daily Beast as "the most shocking scandal of corruption in the history of the NYPD," the criminality and corruption of Michael Dowd, Ken Eurell, and a crew of drug-dealing cops as a gang unto themselves in East New York's 75th Precinct doesn't smell like a rose. To

1

understand it, we must know the soil from which it grew, the culture and attitudes that gave it life, and, for the first time, experience it not only from the perspective of the ethically challenged participants, but also from the perspective of the women who loved them and overlooked their faults—wives who first enjoyed the fruits of their husbands' criminality and then shared the suffering of public shame and ignominious humiliation.

How we hooked up with Ken Eurell is a cool story. Ken Eurell, who had a brief career as one of the most corrupt cops in the history of New York City, sold movie rights to his story to SONY Pictures, but he kept the literary rights.

Ken knew he wasn't an author any more than he was a movie maker. He turned to the excellent Tampa, Florida, journalist and author Paul Guzzo, and Paul suggested that Ken and I should talk.

Excited about the project, I called Frank C. Girardot, Jr, the brilliant, award-winning journalist who co-wrote our best-selling true crime book, *A TASTE FOR MURDER*. He was immediately on board with equal enthusiasm.

Frank and I decided to tell you this story as if you were sitting right here with us, leaning back in your chair or sitting on the edge of your seat.

### 'Let us come to an agreement ...'

When Frank and I write a book, we start with the firm belief that you are our friend. You love true stories, and we have a true story to tell.

To our surprise and delight, two infamous international criminals contacted us directly to share their insights and observations having been there themselves. We're talking about men feared by their enemies, admired by their friends, once hunted by the FBI and INTERPOL, and whose enterprises dealt in all manner of self-indulgence or self-destruction depending upon your genetic makeup and social situation.

Why would a feared former drug lord and a retired international jewel thief, often heavy-handed and notoriously tight-lipped, speak candidly to your two new favorite authors?

Simple. They get to do what they have always wanted to do: set the record straight by telling the true story of their lives and crimes, and assure their place in history by watering their legend and seeing it grow while they are still alive to enjoy it.

Here then is a sweeping epic embracing not only the Dowd-Eurell "Cocaine Cops" corruption scandal of the 1980s, but also the significant precursors from the sepia tone days of historic New York when gaslights lit the streets, cocaine and heroin were perfectly legal, bordellos boasted of the beauty and refinement of their affordable females, and the police force was just another gang amongst many.

This is also—cue the solo piano—an intimate character-driven story of true love, sincere friendship, absolute loyalty, and the heartbreak of betrayal. And yes, the story also has—cue the violins—romance, adorable children, a dog, and an abiding appreciation for time-honored traditions.

Men traditionally communicate to share data; women communicate to share how they feel about the data. One is "law" while the other is "spirit." One is "works," the other is "faith." The crime and corruption in the 75th Precinct of the 1980s is a "man's story," heavy on the testosterone, hold the quinoa and kale. Where were the women? Sure, the men could tell you dates, places, and the names of cops and cadavers, but women are the harmonic/hormonal combination lightning rod and emotional content barometer. Hence, we invited the wives and lovers to share their memories and perspectives on the infectious nature of corruption.

Corruption is dishonest behavior by those in positions of power, such as police or government officials. Corruption can include giving or accepting bribes, planting evidence, creating false confessions, under-the-table transactions, manipulating elections, diverting funds, laundering money, and other illegal acts. An act may be morally reprehensible, but not illegal. If it isn't illegal, it isn't corruption. The law must be broken in order for it to be corruption. There is a hell of a lot of corruption in this story, but no laws were broken in the writing of this book.

## Disclaimer:

As with all true crime books, this is one version of events recalled from memory and adapted from personal in-depth interviews with diverse individuals—information shared by law enforcement, attorneys, private detectives, and other journalists eager to share their observations and opinions.

Any errors of fact are unintentional, some names have been changed to protect privacy, and certain conversations or comments required emendation and speculative reconstruction for your ease of reading and comprehension. Someone else may tell the story differently, but we are not someone else.

Essentially facts are facts, and if we are not 100 percent accurate in some of our interpretations and peripheral details, at least we acknowledge we gave it our best shot. Please promise that after reading this book you won't say or do anything to hurt our feelings. We are dewy-eyed innocents whose only source of joy is seeing you happy.

# CHAPTER 1. THE CHAMPAGNE OF DRUGS

Some know it as coke, snow, yayo, or flake. Others might refer to it as rock, crack, base, or blow.

Call it what you will, but the white powder first derived from a leafy green South American plant in 1859 is best known by its clinical name: cocaine. Sigmund Freud extolled its virtues. It was a key ingredient in Coca-Cola soft drink. Then in 1914 the United States declared cocaine illegal.

Just like everything else that's illegal, coke has never been hard to get.

If you were a party person in the late 1970s or early 1980s you may have put a pile of coke on a mirror, got out a razor blade or credit card, chopped up the coke, and set it out in long white lines. You probably rolled up a dollar bill, stuck it up your nose, bent over the mirror, and inhaled.

Maybe you, or someone you knew, rubbed a little on the gums as a finisher, or dabbed the moist filter of a cigarette in the remains, or applied it to male genitals to prolong sexual performance by delaying orgasm. Yes, that white powder had dozens of household uses. And although cocaine was and is only legal within appropriate medical settings, such as the use of it as an anesthetic, it was considered a benign and friendly recreational drug of little or no danger, until a cheap form of it was used in the 1980s by people of color.

A decade earlier, in the 1970s, cocaine was viewed as a high-class mild intoxicant well suited for the upwardly mobile. A 1974 feature in *The New York Times Sunday Magazine* had the headline, "Cocaine: The Champagne of Drugs." In 1977, *Newsweek* compared the drug to Dom Perignon and caviar. Peter Bourne, President Carter's drug advisor, described cocaine as "benign." The Drug Abuse Council, a Washington think-tank, said cocaine was "like fine wine or liqueur for special occasions." A 1981 *TIME* cover showed a martini glass filled with cocaine. The white powdered stimulant wasn't considered particularly dangerous nor was its use regarded as deviant. In the pantheon of problems facing America at that time, drug use didn't even make the list of important issues or serious problems.

But a change was on the horizon—more specifically in the New York harbor. Reporters sniffed it out first. In August of that year, *CBS News* reporter Steve Young told news audiences the following:

"Authorities say there's an avalanche of cocaine crossing our borders. Just one month before the tall ship Gloria from Columbia, South America, graced New York harbor during the bicentennial celebration she was stopped and 13 pounds of cocaine were found on board.

"Although that stash was worth about $3 million, it amounted to just a trickle of the total cocaine smuggled into the US—by one estimate a ton a week," Young breathlessly began emphasizing the first syllable as in CO-caine.

"Most cocaine comes from South America frequently hidden in ingenious ways, for example tucked inside chocolate bars or diluted in bottles of sherry. Seizures have risen steadily."

The story relied on expert commentary from Peter Benzinger of the fledgling Drug Enforcement Agency who pointed a finger squarely at the growing presence of Columbia in the CO-caine trade.

"These criminal organizations responsible for smuggling cocaine into the United States are big criminals. Don't fool yourself. They recruit fast jet planes, tankers that come up from Columbia. I would say it's a billion-dollar business."

If it were not before, it would be soon enough. A proliferation of addicts helped. Cocaine has a unique power over its users.

*New York Times* columnist David Carr famously wrote about his 1980s cocaine addiction in the book *The Night of the Gun.*

"Once in the noggin, coke calls its own frantic tune, with all the amps turned up to 11. ... It is, for want of a better metaphor, akin to scoring the winning touchdown in the final game of a championship season, and them reliving that moment over and over until the rush ebbs."

When smoked, cocaine releases dopamine "the lingua franca of the pleasure impulse," Carr explained.

Crack is even better.

"Rather than the gradual ride up from powered cocaine, crack makes it happen immediately and profoundly. Senses are more acute, pupils dilate, blood pressure and body temperature rise, and you feel like the lord of all you survey, even if it is a crappy couch and a nonworking television in a dope house."

By the time the 1980s rolled around, suddenly cocaine wasn't so glamorous—especially in the formerly tolerant media—and that's largely because cocaine was now being sold on the streets as crack.

Some say that what happened in the 1980s was, when studied in retrospect, a well-orchestrated "moral panic" of manufactured nonsense, bullshit, and scare tactics about crack cocaine for the purpose of passing repressive and punitive legislation aimed at the poor.

In their book, *Policing the Crisis: Mugging, The State, and Law and Order*, Stuart Hall and his coauthors Chas Chitcher, Tony Jefferson, John Clarke, and Brian Roberts detailed the telltale signs of a manufactured moral panic:

1. When the official reaction is out of all proportion to

the actual threat.

2. When "experts," in the form of police chiefs, the judiciary, politicians, and editors perceive the threat in all but identical terms and appear to talk "with one voice."

3. When the media representations universally stress "sudden and dramatic" increases in the situation.

Crack is essentially cocaine which can be smoked and was developed as an alternative to marijuana following the return of repressive marijuana laws. It came to America and became quite popular, and according to a former FBI sub-contractor, it was intentionally promoted in America's ghettos to insure an ongoing "prisoner class" of citizens to arrest, prosecute, and fill our ever-expanding for-profit prisons.

As the furor over crack in the inner city ramped up, President Ronald Reagan gave speeches warning more and more of the crisis, and other politicians followed his lead. The mayor of New York City, Ed Koch, urged that the death penalty be imposed on any drug dealer convicted for the possession of at least a kilogram of cocaine. A few months after him, the governor of New York, Mario Cuomo, suggested that a life sentence should be given to anyone convicted of selling $50 worth of crack.

Nancy Reagan's office gave America the "Just Say No" campaign which stigmatized the casual drug user as an "accomplice to murder."

As the legal scholar Michelle Alexander noted, "In an effort to secure funding for the new war, Reagan actually hired staff in 1985 to publicize the emergence of crack cocaine in crime-infested neighborhoods."

The propaganda expanded, and more organizations were created with the aim of "raising awareness": College Challenge, World Youth against Drug Abuse, The Just Say

No Club, PRIDE, STOPP, Responsible Adolescents Can Help, Youth to Youth, and Partnership for a Drug-Free America.

"What one can find really amusing about these organizations," wrote sociologist Dimitar Panchev, "is that soon after the end of the moral panic all of them folded and even ceased to exist!"

It may have been a "crisis" to exploit for lawmakers, but it was also a "craze" to exploit for those who sold the drug. Dealers were getting millions of dollars in free advertising every day via radio, television, and print.

Coke was everywhere, and folks from Manhattan to Santa Monica were snorting, smoking, or shoving it up their butts to get high.

"Everybody was on drugs, everybody was fucked up," one New York resident recalled in a documentary directed by Al Profit. "One out of five families had someone who was earning a good living with it."

That "everybody" included a hell of a lot of cops of the NYPD.

In the 1980s, outside of Wall Street, there were two sure ways to make big bucks in the Big Apple: sell drugs or rob drug dealers. The main characters in this story did both, and they weren't worried about the cops, because they were the cops. Drug dealers with a badge, criminals in a squad car, the "Cocaine Cops" of the NYPD were the most powerful drug gang in Brooklyn. This is their story.

# CHAPTER 2. KNOCK, KNOCK. WHO'S THERE?

Ken and Dori Eurell, an attractive couple in their late twenties, lived an idyllic life in the town of Babylon on the edge of Long Island in Suffolk County, far from New York's inner-city slums.

Ken and Dori were the picture perfect couple. Their two-story Hi-Ranch house was graced with the sitcom laughter and antics of two toddlers and oft neurotic behavior of their dog Rocco, an attack-trained rottweiler. In the spotless driveway were a Lincoln LSC and a fire-engine red Corvette convertible. Out back were a red-brick patio, a two-story deck, and an in-ground pool.

They married in the mid-1980s when the couple convinced Dori's father that a nice Jewish girl and a nice Catholic boy who came from opposite sides of the tracks could live happily ever after on Long Island.

Ken grew up in a staunchly Roman Catholic home in Rosedale, Queens, nestled in the heart of a neighborhood filled with the descendants of Irish and Italian immigrants—most of whom held blue collar jobs. The neighborhood was one of those places in the 1960s that was notorious for its ability to produce fighters, drinkers, and con artists. His dad was a no-nonsense working class man who expected his sons to toe the line.

Of Puerto Rican and Jewish heritage, Dori grew up in Five Towns, a grouping of tiny hamlets, just over the border from Queens, on the south shore of Long Island. She was technically from Woodmere. The neighborhood was close enough to Manhattan that her father was able to commute to the East Village six days a week.

"It was the first town right after the city," Dori recalled. "The neighborhood was just the opposite of Ken's. Everyone was a doctor or a lawyer or in a white collar profession. I totally rebelled against it. I didn't like the entitlement of my classmates who believed they were better than everyone else."

When Dori met Ken, that was it. He was the man for her. "I was totally enamored with him," Dori said. "I was totally and completely in love. Everything he said I believed."

By 1992, Ken, a former Brooklyn beat cop, was a satisfied stay-at-home dad receiving a retirement pension from the NYPD, and Dori had a career as a dental assistant.

Ken kept a diary.

> Being Mr. Mom to the family agrees with me. I love being at home taking care of and spending time with my kids. On the outside it appears to all those around me everything is perfect and I have the upper hand in life. In truth, my life is going ninety miles an hour down a dead-end street. If we crash it will be painful as hell -- not only for me -- but also for Dori.

That life-altering, full-blown crisis hit Dori and Ken on what seemed a perfectly normal night in Babylon. Ken was out at a friend's place and would be back soon. Dori had just put the kids down to bed, and she flipped on the tube to watch the Rodney King riots live from Los Angeles, thousands of miles away. The city was in flames that night. Not much else mattered on the news.

There was a knock on the door. Dori wasn't expecting company, and Ken had his own keys. "I was in our upstairs bedroom at the time," Dori remembered, "so I took a peek out the window to see who was there."

That's when things got strange—really, really strange.

"The entire house was surrounded by cops with guns, there were even cops in the bushes with guns," recalled Dori. "It made no sense. Why? What? There's nothing going on in my house. I didn't call the cops."

Dori descended the stairs. Rocco barked at the strangers outside.

"We have a warrant," an officer shouted through the door. "We have a dog," Dori shouted back.

That could have been interpreted as a declaration of parity or superiority, but it

was simply courtesy.

"I can put the dog in another room," Dori offered to the gun-carrying men on the porch and those hiding in the bushes. "Can I put the dog away?"

"Uh … yes, please," said the officer.

The barking and commotion awoke Dori's little girl who found sleepy-eyed comfort out of bed resting on her mom's hip. Her son slept through it all. With the dog sequestered in another room, Dori Eurell opened the door.

"The cops came pouring in, guns drawn, as if on a mission or some sort of raid," Dori recalled, with a slight catch in her voice as she held back the tears that often accompany the memory. "They were running from room to room, looking for God-knows-what."

One cop raced into the room where Dori's husband played video games with his kids, grabbed a piece of paper, and victoriously proclaimed, "I found it, I found it," waving the paper proudly in front of the mystified Mrs. Eurell. The paper contained what appeared to be an elaborate code.

"Do you *realize* what this is?" This wasn't a question; it was a rhetorical challenge.

"Yeah," Dori answered honestly, "I *realize* that those are stats and codes my husband wrote down that go with the video baseball game he plays with our son."

"Oh."

Ken's diary, more of a handwritten memoir, might have given Dori a clue as to why the cops were there. It was missed in the search. Instead the one hundred or so pages were scattered around the bedroom like confetti. A kitchen napkin that doubled as a ledger for Ken's business was also overlooked.

The police furiously tossed the house while Dori paced around holding her overtired yet semi-awake offspring. Dori thought it weird that none of these cops explained why they were in her house, what they were looking for, or anything. Hell, they didn't even ask her name or ask about her husband. Dori was never shy, and she figured she had a right to know what the hell was going on.

"Excuse me …" Dori called out, attempting to get someone's attention. "Excuse me. Will someone please tell me what's this all about? Where's Kenny?"

The phone rang. One of the cops answered it. It was someone asking for Kenny.

"Kenny's not here."

Click.

Dori, dazed and confused, again asked, "What is this all about? Where's my husband, Kenny?"

"Your husband?

"Yes, my husband, Ken Eurell."

"He's under arrest. I suggest you find some child care; you're leaving with us."

"It was so horrible, so unreal," said Dori, "I still didn't get the big picture. I started crying, and I mean really sobbing. That's when they put handcuffs on me."

Ken's arrest in the home of a Long Island friend was also

dramatic. He would eventually add the story to his memoir:

> At 10:30 p.m. I stopped by to pick up money from Harry Vahjen. Vahjen's house was full of customers. I walked into the back bedroom. Vahjen and another guy were cutting and packing product. Suffolk detectives must have been waiting for me to show up because at 10:40 p.m. the SWAT team broke in the front door of Vahjen's house.
> At first I thought we were being robbed. But as soon as I saw the SWAT shields and the uniforms I just placed my hands on the wall. The officer searching me was all excited, pulling a gun from the small of my back. Vahjen was quickly taken into a different room. I suppose he did what we would all do in that same situation. In my mind he was cooperating.

The deputies slapped cuffs on Ken's wrists and dragged him away from the mound of sparkling mother-of-pearl opalescent cocaine sitting on the table nearby.

"This place smells like a dentist's office," remarked one Suffolk County cop apparently unaware that his statement was a compliment, and a testament to the high quality of Ken Eurell's cocaine. As part of "Operation Loser," a cocaine distribution interdiction, Suffolk County arrested dozens of others that night. Among them were low-level users and mid-level dealers. A couple of kingpins were hooked up as well.

The next morning, the proud and effusive Suffolk County detectives behind "Operation Loser" put guns, drugs, and other evidence on display for the media. They announced the results of "Operation Loser," and dropped a bombshell: former and current New York City police officers were selling drugs in the suburbs. Among the suspects were NYPD Officer Michael Dowd, a mustachioed and double chinned smart-aleck, and his retired partner, now stay-at-home dad Ken Eurell.

Within hours, the biggest drug and corruption scandal in the history of the NYPD had become national news.

## CHAPTER 3. NYPD DNA

*"The NYPD today is a much larger, more professional, and better-trained organization than it was in the 1890s. Now, as then, the great majority of police are dedicated civil servants rather than crooked predators."* — **Daniel Czitrom, *TIME* Magazine**

Police scandals cause significant damage to a city because they involve those we would regard as our protectors. It is as if your parent or a beloved uncle abused you. Each successive betrayal is another trauma, and the cumulative effect of repeated police scandals becomes part of a city's self-image. As with all forms of abuse, it is most often perpetuated generation after generation.

Kenny Eurell wasn't the only law enforcement associate arrested in the Suffolk County round-up. Detectives also arrested his former partner Mike Dowd and several other on-duty police officers.

While Kenny was merely around coke, Dowd had it in his bloodstream; he was high and drunk when he was booked.

This was a news story that had legs. Reporters crawled up and down Long Island looking for stories about Ken and Dori.

They staked out Ken's house. They rang the doorbell at Dowd's elaborate mansion on Long Island. Reporters attended the hearings, the arraignments; they pulled the paperwork and followed the money. They scratched the surface and wrote broad, cartoonish paragraphs about booze-fueled orgies, late-night runs to Atlantic City, Columbian connections, and sinister missing persons cases.

Bit by bit, reporters at the *Post*, the *Daily News*, *Newsday*, and *The New York Times* pieced together some elements of the real story. And readers who followed the news through headlines got a broad sense of what was wrong in the city. The New York tabloids, in the midst of a circulation war, went wild. For days after the busts, lurid all-caps headlines shouted at subway commuters: "COCAINE COPS"; THE HOUSE THAT COKE BUILT; ROGUE COPS; PSYCHO COP; COPS KIDNAPPED DRUG DEALER; SUSPECT COP ALSO EYED IN SLAYING AND HOLD-UP; SCORE OF A LIFTIME.

The jumps and back pages held more details; some were incredible, others mundane.

For sure it was a barnburner. If the newspapers were to be believed, East New York's Seven Five Precinct was a hotbed for thievery, treachery, murder, cover-up, and corruption, and Kenny and Mike were in the thick of the shitstorm.

Pictures of the two filled the gap between razor thin copy rife with speculation and advertisements. When the papers had more space, sometimes the layouts included pictures of cocaine bricks or menacing guns. It was, after all, part of the story.

Another component of the story bubbling to the surface was the fact that it took a group of Barney Fife deputies in Podunk Suffolk County to arrest the bad boy cops from the ghetto.

Say what? Who dropped the ball on that one?

As for the other characters? The way the cop reporters told the tale there were drug dealers bigger than Tony Montana and cops as noble as Serpico involved in this thing. It was clear Kenny and Mike weren't doing their dirt alone or even in the dark. And the corruption wasn't just in the Seven Five. Shit. It was pervasive. All over the NYPD. Eventually some adult somewhere would have to assess what happened.

Editorials called on the NYPD to investigate itself. Hand-wringing opinion writers questioned where the NYPD went wrong. Didn't Serpico put a stop to all of this? Should we pay police more? Where was Internal Affairs? How did this slip through the cracks?

The headlines might as well have screamed, WHAT'S WRONG WITH OUR SOCIETY?

There might have been a thousand or more unanswered questions in those weeks following the arrests of Mike Dowd, Kenny Eurell, and their crew. Some might have been answered, but it would have required looking at the past of the New York City Police Department to explain the crisis.

Had some intrepid investigator gone back and looked, he or she would have found previous examples of every sort of bad conduct Mike Dowd and Ken Eurell were accused of having engaged in. The New York Police Department owes its very existence to scandal. The bureaucracy of the very same department can claim to be viable because it grew out of reform. And the papers that covered it all? Well, the editors and reporters might have changed, but the elements of a good tale have always remained the same.

## The Cycle Begins

One might have argued that Ken and Mike were the latest players in a cycle of scandal and reform that began all the way back in 1840 with the murder of Helen Jewett.

Jewett's real name was Dorcas Doyan. She was one of eight beautiful, erudite, and charming women working in a Thomas Street bordello managed by Ms. Rosina Townsend. Every aspect of the enterprise bespoke upscale excellence, luxurious ambiance, and a firm assurance of customer satisfaction.

Expensive Turkish rugs lined the floors, each room had

beveled-glass mirrors, and the women, regarded as the most beautiful prostitutes in the nation, were well loved by an endless stream of customers coming at all hours.

So excellent was the bordello's reputation that the four New York City "watchmen" sent to Thomas Street the night Jewett was murdered assumed they were headed to an incident that contained nothing more serious than two clients fighting over the same woman. They were ill-prepared emotionally or professionally for what the crime scene revealed: the lithe and lovely Helen Jewett, her head cleaved open by an ax and half of her body burned in a fire that smoldered for hours in thick winter covers.

The shocking scene did little to change the cops' unprofessional protocol. The male clientele was allowed to leave; the women were largely ignored. Despite their amateur efforts, investigators stumbled upon sufficient clues to deduce that the killer fled out the back door and climbed a recently whitewashed fence. His hasty exit smeared the paint.

Other physical evidence, including the bloody hatchet and a cloak, soon led police to a boarding house and a suspect: Richard Robinson, the nineteen-year-old son of a wealthy Connecticut farmer. Robinson's pants were stained with white paint, he owned the abandoned cloak, and his frequent visits to the victim for sexual pleasures, including that very night, were all strong indications that he was the culprit.

A coroner's inquest took place that afternoon, and the men who conducted the inquiry immediately concluded that Robinson murdered Jewett. There was a speedy trial in which Mr. Robinson was identified by the other women as a customer of Ms. Jewett that evening, and his freshly whitewashed stained pants were paraded for the jury.

Thanks to the recent invention of the telegraph,

newspapers around the nation carried sensationalized stories during Robinson's trial about "the wickedest city in the world." Like they did for Kenny and Mike nearly 150 years later, reporters dug up every sordid detail of Jewett's personal life from conditions of her childhood, upbringing, and her procession of locations, to lurid allusions to Jewett's lucrative career as one of New York's finest sexually adept courtesans.

When readers' interest in the story flagged, reporters included made-up details of the gruesome crime scene and created a storyline that hinted at a love affair between Robinson and Jewett outside the confines of the bordello. One thing the reporters got right? Their characterizations of the fairly worthless group of volunteer watchmen who investigated the slaying.

Despite the blood, guts, sex, and death contained in the Jewett tragedy, a jury of twelve men reached its unanimous and easily predicted verdict within minutes of the trial's close: Not Guilty.

In an oft-repeated display of editorial handwringing, newspapers expressed outrage that the murder went unsolved and that the real killer was out there somewhere. Hence, the credit or blame for the birth of the NYPD as we know it today goes to the "unsolved murder" of Helen Jewett.

Following the botched trial, as they would in Ken and Mike's case, reformers demanded change. What they got was a professional police department.

In 1845 New York City hired 1,200 men to police New York's 320,000 residents. Anything involving the hiring and paying of 1,200, plus the administration of their duties, had to be a magnetic force attracting political power struggles and opportunistic corruption. It wouldn't take long for the cycle of corruption, exposure, and reform to repeat itself.

Early on, the combatants were the Democrats of

Tammany Hall who ran the city, and the state's powerful Republicans. The NYPD became more professional, and it also became more brutal. Beatings were commonplace. Graft was rife. Appointment to the force depended on connections. A bureaucracy, that remained largely intact in the 1990s, began to take shape.

Promotion through the ranks required payoffs to superior officers. To be made a patrolman cost $300. A promotion to sergeant ran $1,400, and advancement to captain cost a whopping $14,000. The cost was covered by taking in bribes.

To be a cop in New York City in the late nineteenth century was akin to being a member of an exclusive fraternity. An initiation ritual, which was nothing more than hazing, involved drinking, painting new recruits green, and a variety of degrading humiliations. New cops were ordered to take a solemn oath.

## 'It's Us Against Them Out There Boy-o'

As Kenny and Mike would explain to authorities a century later, cops were taught about the "Blue Wall" that separated them from the citizenry.

Under no circumstances were sworn NYPD officers to reveal department secrets. Informant cops—known as noses, rats, and snitches—were looked upon as pariahs and shunned by their peers.

A veteran advising a rookie about how to get along on the job would tell him to express no opinions on religion or politics, take his hazing like a man, never rat on his comrades, and—the key to acceptance—rush forward with club swinging, no questions asked, to back up another cop who was in trouble.

A refrain rose among those officers who knew the real score: "It's us against them out there boy-o."

Oftentimes the corruption/exposure/reform cycle that formed the modern NYPD had its roots in bare-knuckle politics. It's a fact that Ken and Mike skated for as long as they did because of politics. No one wanted to rock the boat. So Dowd's crew was left to its own devices. What resulted were thefts, stickups, and dope dealing.

As the nineteenth century gave way to the twentieth, the power plays between the Republicans upstate and the city Democrats increased, and the Republicans found a peg on which to hang their oppositional identity. It wasn't murder and grand theft that bothered them, it was immorality.

Murder, rape, and theft are assuredly immoral, but when the stage is politics you perform a play about behavior you can pretend to control: other people's sex lives and their recreational intoxications.

People drinking, drugging, and having sex could only happen, asserted the state's Republican Party, if the police department were corrupt. With an election looming on the horizon, the New York State Republicans were now shocked at New York City being a Democrat-controlled den of alcoholic iniquity, promiscuous vice, unholy temptation, and carnal smut. In other words, it was New York.

## Lather, Rinse, Repeat

The outrage of self-proclaimed clean living and highly moral Republicans focused not on crime prevention or harm reduction, but in 1894 zealously created the first of many commissions—the Lexow Commission—to investigate vice-based corruption in the NYPD.

The Lexow Commission's primary target was Police Chief William Devery, known as the "King of Kickbacks." Devery, a wax-mustachioed, blustering bon vivant with a receding hairline and an expanding belly, looked like a body double for President Grover Cleveland, but he was one of a kind as New York's top cop.

Devery was one of those love 'em or hate 'em types. He engendered strong reactions of derision from his detractors in the state capital and equally strong feelings of admiration from the men who worked by his side. Of course they admired him—he increased their personal material well-being in exchange for devaluing their ethics. The respect was mutual as long as his acolytes observed the unofficial code of the NYPD—keep your hand out and your mouth shut.

When he first took command of a lower East Side precinct, Devery exclaimed, "They tell me there's a lot of grafting going on in this precinct. They tell me you fellows are the fiercest ever on graft. Now that's going to stop! If there's any grafting to be done, I'll do it. Leave it to me."

No matter how crooked the scheme or how cooked the book, nothing stuck to this dapper chief of police. In the words of journalist Lincoln Steffens, "As chief of police he is a disgrace, but as a character he is a work of art."

His personal charisma equaled his corruption, and all that resulted from the months of interrogation. The resultant five-volume, 10,000-word report on the ills of the Democrat's Tammany Hall machine and its allies in uniform was one concise and accurate evaluation of the NYPD of 1894:

*"The members of the Police Department were bound together by ... the cohesion of public plunder. They were not of the people. They did not belong to the people. They regarded themselves as separate and apart from the people."*

Once again, the refrain "It's us against them out there boy-o" was repeated.

The theme would be echoed in official investigations through the next century.

The Lexow investigation resulted in almost half of the entire NYPD facing indictments on charges of bribery, extortion, and neglect of duty.

Three years later, not one New York police official went to jail, and everyone kicked off the force was reinstated with back pay. So much for the legendary reputation of Theodore Roosevelt, who was appointed as the new commissioner of the NYPD.

Roosevelt attempted riding roughshod over Devery's loyal minions but found his charges frustrated and defeated. Never one to shy away from a publicity and public relations opportunity, Roosevelt invented his own heroic legend by volunteering to fight in the Spanish American War—a conflict created by media mogul William Randolph Hearst to sell newspapers.

Returning a celebrity, Roosevelt was elected vice president in 1906. When President William McKinley died at the hands of an assassin, Roosevelt became president. Both McKinley and New York police reforms were buried the same day.

## Mobsters, Muscle, and Money

As the newspaper stories would allege in the early 1990s, Mike Dowd and Kenny Eurell consorted with mobsters and gunmen. It was really nothing new among NYPD officers.

Take the story of gangster Big Jack Zelig. It was easy for him to rise to a position of power in gangland New York because he had the protection of NYPD's Charles Becker, a police lieutenant who earned excessive amounts of money by turning a blind eye to Zelig's criminal activities.

The New York press referred to Becker and his two fellow detectives as The Strong Arm Squad.

Becker's squad would raid "suspicious locations"— mostly enterprises not paying protection money to Becker. Planting guns and planting evidence was Plan A; killing the non-paying criminals was Plan B.

The squad also provided protection to roulette and faro parlors. Typically, a member of the squad would work outside security, rousting potential troublemakers and accepting entrance fees from big spenders.

Big Jack Zelig was a bad dude. He practically pioneered the drive-by murder and a host of other modern urban terror techniques. Jack was doing it in the name of consolidating his operation, and he was thankful to have a cop on the payroll in much the same way certain drug dealers would be thankful for the services of Kenny and Mike eight decades later.

Zelig hooked up with Becker and began providing the Strong Arm Squad with the names of competing Lower East Side bookmakers. Members of Becker's squad would bust up the operations of Zelig's competitors, get some juice, pass up the proper amount to their supervisors, and keep the peace—all at the same time.

The heat of the Strong Arm Squad could be intense. Take the case of Herman "Beansy" Rosenthal, a Zelig competitor. Rosenthal felt he was being squeezed too tight and complained to the *New York World* newspaper.

When a story on his scam appeared in the newspaper, Becker was so pissed off that he hired hit men to kill Rosenthal. The result? Beansy was gunned down in a drive-by shooting that had all the earmarks of a Zelig-engineered hit.

Ultimately Becker was arrested and tried for his role in the murder. Sentenced to the electric chair, Becker has the distinction of being the only New York Police officer executed for his crimes.

One of the men on the fringes of the Lower East Side's Jewish gangs was "Yiddy Jack" Albert. He had pals in the legendary Eastman Gang, but following the death of Zelig and the frying of Becker, Yiddy Jack decided that one could reap rewards from the criminals' proclivities without indulging in criminal activities.

Opening a bare knuckles boxing gym in the neighborhood allowed him a respectable career while maintaining at least a tangential relationship with well-heeled hoodlums. Boxing, after all, has always been among the most tolerated of corrupted competitions.

## Beau James

If the NYPD were merely dysfunctional in the eighteenth century and benignly corrupt in the nineteenth century, it was downright criminal in the twentieth. Early on the corruption stemmed right from the top.

Take the case of Mayor Jimmy Walker. A sharp-chinned, red-nosed charmer with a well-coifed (if receding) hairline, Walker was fond of fur-lined winter coats that had a pocket for his monogrammed silk handkerchief. On his left hand, Walker, aka Beau James, wore a large gold pinkie ring. His right hand was often adorned with a cigarette holder that was often adorned with an unlit cigarette. Walker, who barely weighed 125 pounds, often designed his own clothes and was known for his custom-made ties. Those who knew Walker, New York's mayor from 1926 until 1932, best described him as a fox, who looked nearly devilish when he'd finally light that cigarette with his monogrammed gold lighter. Walker was not only colorful and outrageous, but also culpable in covertly sanctioning all manner of wrongdoing. He sang, he danced, and he lived it up, but he never lived up to his anti-vice campaign rhetoric.

"I like the company of my fellow human beings. I like the theatre and am devoted to healthy outdoor sports. Because I like these things," said Walker. "I have reflected my attitude in some of my legislation I have sponsored 2.75 percent beer, Sunday baseball, Sunday movies, and legalized boxing. But let me allay any fear there may be that, because I believe in personal liberty, wholesome amusement, and healthy professional sport, I will not countenance for a moment any indecency or vice in New York."

As one wise wag commented, "Everyone bought it, but no one believed it."

Walker, who was selling judgeships and doling out city money like he was printing it himself, eventually fled the country. Like his cousin Theodore two decades earlier, Governor Franklin Roosevelt pursued Walker's case and found his way into the White House as a result of the scandal. FDR didn't really put a stop to anything.

In the 1950s, NYPD officials pledged a complete overhaul and promised reformed self-policing. More about optics than authenticity, they turned a blind eye to street-level corruption and overlooked the endemic dishonesty.

## A Rat, a Best Seller, and a Golden Globe

To outside appearances, the NYPD had once and for all reformed. The inward reality, however, assured a scandal loomed in the offing. In the early 1970s, America would learn of Detective Frank Serpico, who, after turning his fellow cops in for corruption, became the subject of a best-selling book and award-winning movie. In the flick, Serpico was famously portrayed by Al Pacino, who won the Golden Globe for his nuanced performance.

Serpico's story didn't only involve drug cops who were shaking down dealers for some quick dough. Even everyday police work had an angle as beat cops would pile traffic tickets on restaurant owners who refused to comp their meals. Frank Serpico laid it all out and was despised by his colleagues for doing it.

Following Serpico's revelations in April 1970, Mayor John Lindsay formed the Knapp Commission to once again examine police corruption in New York City.

Not much had changed from the days of Devery and Becker. Patrolmen collected the bribe money and passed it up the chain in a pyramid scam of sorts that didn't pay off for rookies until they proved they were not going to rat or snitch.

Knapp attempted to explain why officers were loyal to one another—even though what they were witnessing in the precinct houses or participating in on the street was absolutely wrong.

"Everyone agrees that a policeman's life is a dangerous one, and that his safety, not to mention his life, can depend on his ability to rely on a fellow officer in a moment of crisis.

To read Knapp is to realize that the New York Police Department of 1970, functioning in Richard Nixon's Silent Majority America, exhibited a weird psychology of denial and co-dependency. Knapp explained the psychology in terms most high school sophomores could understand.

"Any policeman found to be corrupt must promptly be denounced as a rotten apple in an otherwise clean barrel."

Such was the heritage and history of the NYPD when Ken Eurell, a good blue collar Catholic with goals of sincere public service, decided to become one of New York's Finest. Ken was a true New Yorker through and through. So was his wife, Dori Albert Eurell, the granddaughter of Yiddy Jack Albert.

# CHAPTER 4. AND YIDDY JACK BEGAT JOSEPH

Yiddy Jack Albert had three sons, the middle boy was named Joseph. Born March 13, 1923, Joseph and his brother ran a check-cashing business. New York of the 1950s and '60s was a different place than it had been a half-century earlier. New high rises obliterated many of the old landmarks, street names had changed, and the demographics swung away from Jewish immigrants to Puerto Ricans and hippies.

The beginning of that postwar change came in 1935. That year "First Houses," New York City's original housing project, was built on the Lower East Side. The development offered 122 apartments featuring oak wood floors and brass fixtures. The rent, adjusted to each family's monthly income, ranged from five to seven dollars a month. The New York City Housing Authority received more than 1,000 applications for the project before it was even complete.

The families that lived there and in the projects that followed were mostly wage earners who eked out an existence paycheck-to-paycheck. By the mid-1960s, the projects were often the last resort for welfare moms, heroin addicts, and drunks. Any green space on the Lower East Side was overrun with garbage.

Rats roamed freely. In less than one hundred years, Manhattan's nicest neighborhood had become one of its most dangerous slums. Dangerous though it was, in the heart of the neighborhood, at 300 East Fifth Street, blue collar guys regularly cashed their checks at Joseph and Sydney's tiny storefront. Because it was the only game in town, Joseph and Sydney had to have a lot of cash on hand—especially at the end of the week.

Perhaps trouble was inevitable. Drug addiction was rampant. Robberies were commonplace and brazen. In the late 1960s, a group of Puerto Rican gang members roaming the neighborhood thought nothing of robbing a Mulberry Street mafia capo at knifepoint. Joseph was targeted often, once losing $150,000 in a stick up. Sydney wound up a causality. Headed to the bank with a load of cash, he was gunned down in 1969. Murder was so commonplace at the time, the story got no mention in *The New York Times*.

"When Sydney died, my dad lost faith in God, and we became just about non-practicing Jews," Dori Albert recalled. "We still did the Jewish holidays, but now they were taken much less serious. I used to talk to him about faith. But I knew my words fell on deaf ears."

On the other side of Dori's family were the Collazos. Her grandfather Louis Collazo was born in Ciales, Puerto Rico. Dori's grandmother Adele Maldonado, also of Puerto Rico, grew up in a rural area just outside of Ciales. She was the eldest of sixteen children and helped raise her siblings.

Adele's father was somewhat of a local legend. Family members said horses he raised and trained were favored by Teddy Roosevelt's Rough Riders and were a key component in the American victory at San Juan Hill, Cuba, during the Spanish American War.

Adele was somewhat of a local hero herself.

"When a flood came through the village she not only saved her brother but also saved four other children in the village," Dori said. "She was a very strong swimmer."

Adele could also sew, which was a blessing and a curse.

"She was a master seamstress doing everything from curtains to my sister Judy's bridal gown." Dori remarked. "She also fabricated most of my clothes throughout my grade school years. To me it was a love/hate relationship with her making my clothes.

"As much as I admired her skill and the care she took in doing so, my fashion was not up to speed in my well-to-do school. Where girls were wearing jeans, I was stuck in these pattern polyester outfits."

Adele and Louis never argued. They loved each other, and they were very religious. Louis, an extremely proud American, loved the United States. He would never say he was Puerto Rican. When asked about his nationality, Louis would reply, "American." Adele began doing the same.

The couple settled in Brooklyn and had one child, DaisyMae, Dori's mother.

While Dori's dad, was a warm, loving, and generous guy who would take her and her twin sister to Nunley's Amusement Park on Long Island, Dori's mother was distant and combative.

DaisyMae grew up in East New York. A stunningly beautiful young woman who enjoyed being a Brooklynite and loved to act tough, DaisyMae attended Thomas Jefferson High School on Pennsylvania Avenue in the heart of the 75th Precinct.

There wasn't much DaisyMae couldn't do. She was an accomplished dancer, a beauty pageant winner, a painter, a porcelain doll maker, a seamstress. In fact, there were very few arts and crafts she didn't master.

DaisyMae met Joseph Albert at a dance. Although sixteen years separated the couple, they were smitten with each other at once. It came together just as DaisyMae attempted to light a cigarette. Joseph didn't smoke but managed to borrow a lighter and got close enough to make the sale.

Beautiful and talented though she was, DaisyMae's personality was edgy at best.

"My mother was, and is, the most beautiful and talented

woman I have ever met," Dori said. "Her one drawback is her hair-trigger temper. She loved being this tough broad. She was also very aware how her beauty affected others. But she loved her husband through and through."

Dori's mom converted to Judaism and took on the name Miriam before she married Joseph. Their children would be brought up Jewish.

Although the murder of his brother caused Joseph to rethink his faith, the family celebrated Passover, Rosh Hashanah, Yom Kippur, and other Jewish high holidays, Dori said. It's just that he didn't take it seriously. That bothered her growing up.

"I wanted to take part and follow the traditions, but there was a lack of attention, to meaning, there was a non-seriousness, I guess you would call it. We still had Passover and everything, but it wasn't taken seriously. There was too much joking going on," Dori recalled. "My dad was still the most incredible, kindest person though. I never heard him curse. He never drank. He was very clean living and very generous."

Ken Eurell met Dori Albert, and each found the other remarkably attractive.

Ken had no trouble winning Dori's heart, but her father was concerned about his daughter marrying a policeman. Ken convinced his future father-in-law that he would be a good husband and a good provider. Upon gaining approval, Ken also received a first-hand taste of Joseph's generous side about the time he and Dori married.

"Kenny was always a saver," said Dori with admiration, "He wanted to be married. He knew what he wanted to do. He saved up $30,000, so that he would have something when it came time to buy a house. My father was impressed by that, and he gave us another $30,000 to get us started."

Ken appreciated his father-in-law's generosity, most

especially because Ken Eurell came from a family of equal strength and work ethic. As with Dori's family, his was also 100 percent proud to be American.

Eurell's father, James, was born in 1933 and raised in Ozone Park Queens. "Big Jim," as he was known, was a twin. After he was drafted in 1956, Big Jim served in the US Army in Germany.

Military service ran in the Eurell blood line. Big Jim's father was a Navy man who raised his family of three sons and a daughter and worked hard at the Brooklyn Navy Yard. During WWII, the elder Eurell was one of nearly 70,000 workers at the Navy Yard putting in over three shifts a day, seven days a week to fit warships for battle in the Atlantic and Pacific.

The Navy Yard, also served as a supply depot for hundreds of ships, and true to New York tradition, the Yard was known for high-profile corruption scandals equal in duplicity and dishonesty to those that afflicted City Hall and the NYPD. No breath of scandal ever touched Big Jim Eurell.

Watching how his own father sweated for hours on the job, Big Jim became a worker bee. Ken said his dad, when a teen, lost blood, sweat, and years on construction jobs that eventually led to employment as a union carpenter.

He worked union construction, framing, roofing, high rise in the city and small homes in the outer boroughs. In the freezing New York winters or under the hot summer sun, my dad would be swinging that hammer to provide for our family. He would work six days a week—and every now and then seven days a week—so my brothers and I wouldn't go without.

When Big Jim retired he had almost fifty years on the job and paid his union dues well into his eighties.

Ken's mother, Esther Siever, born in 1938, the eldest of four children, was a Jew of European descent who grew up in Richmond Hill, Queens, in an attached home at the last stop of the A Train at 118th Street and Liberty Avenue. Much to her family's dismay and amazement, Esther converted to Catholicism while a young adult, and took to her newfound faith with all the zeal of a convert.

Esther was employed as a bookkeeper who took the train into Manhattan every day, including the first five years of Ken's life, for her job. As a result, Ken was actually raised by his grandmother.

The 1960s was a time when a five-year-old kid could safely walk alone on Liberty Avenue. Ken was that kid. Most days he would run from his grandmother's house to meet his mother as she stepped off the El. As a robust kindergartener, Ken frequently walked alone the ten blocks from P.S. 100 to his grandmother's home after school.

The path home often took Ken past the neighborhood firehouse where firefighters attached to Engine Company 308 lived and worked. The red-brick, two-story fire house with its thick red garage door was ornamented with an outsized American flag and a plaque proclaiming its importance in the neighborhood and society. It served as a reminder of the role law enforcement and first responders play in the community, and New York in the early 1960s, in spite of its sprawling footprint was really not much more than a collection of tight-knit, patriotic, and God-fearing neighborhoods.

Being raised in Richmond Hill was short-lived. The growing Eurell family moved to Rosedale after Big Jim bought his first house. Where Richmond Hill is practically in the heart of Queens, Rosedale is practically in the next county. Entering Rosedale on Francis Lewis Boulevard one is immediately notified that law enforcement is present by a sign stating: "Entering Rosedale. Patrolled by N.Y. Finest Police and Rosedale Civilian Patrol."

Once I entered the first grade, mom quit her high-paying city gig and volunteered in the office at St. Clare, the private Catholic school we went to growing up. My classmates and I were going to confession every week so we could make our first Holy Communion with a clean soul.

"Tell me your sins my son," the priest would say.

I was six. I had no sins.

"Surely you must have some sin to tell me my son. ..."

It was dark and scary in there at six years old. I just wanted to get out. So now I'm lying to the priest to shut him up. Every week I prepared a lie to tell the priest so that I could get out of there quickly.

The Eurells rapidly assimilated into their new neighborhood. Soon kids from all over the neighborhood flocked to the family's house.

Our dad was never too tired to throw the ball around with us in the backyard. Always helping out our little league teams coaching.

Anytime Big Jim came out on top in the weekly poker game, Ken and his brothers benefitted.

When he would win he was always placing
money on the top of our dressers so we
could find it the next morning.

Finding money atop dressers would become a signature
move for Ken and his future partner in law enforcement
Mike Dowd.

Ken and Mike didn't know each other in the '60s, but
their home lives couldn't be more different. Ken's family
was united, loving, and mutually supportive. Dowd's family,
according to his wife, Bonnie, never gave little Michael the
kind of love, acceptance, and encouragement that he needed
and wanted.

"Ken and Mike were, in some ways, entirely different
in terms of approach and presentation, yet they meshed
perfectly in their endeavors," recalls Pavle Stanimirovic, a
man who would run in the circles of those who ran circles
around law enforcement.

"When I say endeavors, I just don't mean criminal ones.
Remember, apart from being bad cops, they were very good
cops. Especially if someone was trying to push you around.
Ken wouldn't stand for that. He despised bullies."

# CHAPTER 5. THE ART OF BULLY CONTROL

By the late 1960s, the Eurell family had grown. Ken was the older brother to John, born in 1964, and Chris who was born in 1967.

I was small for my age, one of the smallest in my classes at any given year. My size never really bothered me, but I would have problems with bullies at times. In grammar school the bully was two years older than me. The school bully didn't just pick fights with kids. He also had confrontations with teachers.

**Eventually the bully would confront Ken.**

One day he dropped his pencil and asked me to pick it up. Instead, I instantly kicked it across the room without thinking about the possible outcome of my action. It seemed like a funny thing to do, and other kids laughed until the bully yelled, "You're dead! After school I'm going to kick your ass!"

Well I didn't back out or run away. The bully and I took the same bus home so there was no running away. Once the bus left so did the only adult who could have prevented a fight. I could have just gotten on the bus and left myself, but being known as a sissy seemed worse than getting beat up.

I was in no way ready for what was about to come. The bully immediately grabbed me by the shirt and punched me three times in the left eye before I even knew what had happened. Instinct made me grab him around the neck and take him to the ground. Maybe fear and self-preservation took over. The bully went home with a bloody nose.

Back at home my pop gave the brothers a talk that night that sticks with me to this day: "I don't care how big or old the other guys are, you help your brother anyway you can. Pick up a stick, a bat, a garbage can, anything."

The "help your brother" ethos resonated deeply when Ken became an adult.

When I heard the same idea put forward about cops being there for other cops, no matter what, it brought back memories of my dad giving us the same advice.

One thing for sure: No matter what, Ken Eurell would never tolerate being bullied—not as a child and certainly not as an adult.

By the time he graduated high school, Ken knew what he wanted—a stable career. But he wasn't sure of how that would happen.

In June of 1978, at seventeen years old, I wasn't sure what I was going to do with my life. But I knew what I didn't want: to work construction with my father. I admired him for doing it every day, but I believed there had to be another way for me.

Ken's parents suggested their son find a career working for the city—good benefits, a pension, and steady work—no matter what the weather had in store.

My mother would pick up a weekly paper that listed all the upcoming civil service exams in New York. In 1979, the NYPD offered the first exam for potential police officers since the massive layoff of 1975.

I went to school two nights a week after work to learn about the cop test. I saw many of my old high school friends at both the school and again on the testing day. I paid the exam application fee and would take the test at John Adams High School in Ozone Park, Queens, which was where my mom went to high school. My dad also knew that neighborhood as it was his old stomping grounds.

Ken was never at the top of his class in high school, instead doing the least he could do and still graduate. With the cop training, however, he had a more committed attitude.

I took it seriously and really applied myself. While my old school buddies were in the parking lot getting high, I went into class and did my best.

Caring about the outcome paid off. Ken scored 98 percent and was ecstatic. His parents had a more reserved "wait and see" response, and his dad felt that Ken, at eighteen years old, was too immature to be a cop.

"Don't worry, Dad," explained Ken, "the minimum hiring age is twenty, so I've got a good two years of physical tests, medical exams, psych evaluations, and background checks. In the meantime, I've still got my job at the stereo shop."

The pay was entry level, but the gear was top of the line. Ken loved spending the day surrounded by the ultimate in professional stereo sound. His employers were firm but kind, and as a minimum wage employee, Ken looked for a career rather than a job.

> At age nineteen I went to work for a Long Island electronics firm. I supervised eight to ten people. I considered this a job that offered me a real future. One I could raise a family on. I worked six days a week. There were some nights a few of us would stay until 10:00 p.m. trying to meet a project deadline. That's a long day considering we started at 7:00 a.m.

An NYPD investigator arranged to meet Ken in November 1980, just after he turned twenty. He said the police department's investigation into Ken's background was nearly complete and if everything checked out Ken would soon be a member of the force.

> On January 23, 1981, I was notified to go to police headquarters on January

26, to be sworn in. It came so quick
I wasn't sure how to tell my friends
and employer that I was leaving in just
three days. There were some tears and a
small good-bye party.

The tiny company's newsletter the next month mentioned
Ken Eurell was off to the NYC Police Academy for six
months of rigorous training. One thing the training didn't
cover with sufficient rigor was the historic fact that your
NYPD shield would not and could not shield you from the
lure of easy money and the temptation to shelve your ethics.

# CHAPTER 6. POLICE ACADEMY

Ronald Reagan was inaugurated as the fortieth president of the United States on January 20, 1981. That same day, fifty-two American hostages held captive in Iran were released and sent home. The timing wasn't a coincidence. Allegedly the hostages would have been home months earlier were it not for the kind of good, old-fashioned backroom bribery that made New York politics famous.

According to a former Iranian president, candidate Ronald Reagan's people went behind President Jimmy Carter's back, cut a deal with Ayatollah Khomeini—the Iranian cleric who led the Iranian Revolution—to hold the hostages until *after* the election.

At the exact moment that Reagan was sworn into office, January 20, 1981, Iran released the hostages and Reagan gave a twenty-minute speech. He made no mention of the backroom deal that helped him defeat the incumbent president, nor did he make any mention of crime or drugs.

Within a few months, however, the Reagan administration shifted funding from health care providers to criminal prosecutors. And while drug addiction was acknowledged as a medical condition rather than a criminal act, Reagan directed law enforcement to arrest and prosecute drug users.

"It's far more effective," said President Reagan, " if you take the customers away than if you try to take the drugs away from those who want to be customers."

During Reagan's administration the average annual amount of funding for eradication and interdiction programs—arresting and prosecuting—increased from an annual average of $437 million during Carter's presidency to $1.4 billion during Reagan's first term, a 1989 Pentagon research project found. That same year also witnessed a New York crime wave punctuated by 2,166 murders and 120,344 robberies. Some of those crimes involved the Mafia and other gang criminals. Most of it appeared utterly senseless and random. The underbelly of New York City in 1981 had more to offer than simple crime and mob assault, and 42nd Street provided sufficient sin and pleasure to have the Republican State Legislature of the 1800s getting graveyard torque from spinning in their graves.

Old theaters were transformed into platforms for live sex acts and XXX movies, while their candy lobbies had taken to selling dildos, blow-up dolls, and amyl nitrate poppers.

Street gangs overran Brooklyn. The Bronx looked more like Beirut than it did a modern American city. Queens witnessed a Gambino Family crime wave directed by mobster John Gotti and his henchmen from the Bergin Hunt and Fish Club in Ozone Park. Staten Island children were targeted by a sex predator.

The year 1981 was only twenty-six days old when Kenny Eurell, age twenty, started his first day on the job at the NYPD, but the decade would see the city's fortunes with drugs, gangs, and crime turn from bad to worse to downright intolerable.

I went to NYPD headquarters at One Police Plaza that day with a friend who lived up the block from me. We were placed in alphabetical order when we arrived. It was a strange experience. I was still so uncertain about what I was even doing there. We were told to raise our right hands and repeat an oath to uphold the law. My heart just didn't seem in it. Maybe it was my age, maybe it was because I didn't always dream of this day like others did.

For the next couple of days we mostly filled out employment and insurance forms in the academy gym on 20th Street in Manhattan. While the majority of new recruits still lived at home with their parents, others had full adult responsibilities.

Some left high-paying jobs because they had the dream of always becoming a police officer. All the younger recruits would tease them, "Why would you leave a job that paid so well?"

In the months of intense training and academic studies, Ken had a great time making new friends, but there was one aspect of the experience that meant the most to twenty-year-old Kenny Eurell.

"Oh, yeah," enthused Ken. "The most important thing was an immediate sense of camaraderie."

As with the thousands of cops before him, Ken Eurell experienced fraternal bonding—forming deep ties with those who entered into a covenant to serve and protect the people of New York.

Well, not exactly.

It was an emotional linkage and near neurotic attachment to those who, like Kenny, would soon see themselves as an exclusive life form, distinct from the general population. This is no different than the sense of security, protection, and bonding experienced by those who join gangs or, for that matter, social service organizations such as the Elks

Club. People united in a common cause, with their purposes harmonized, and characterized by the concept of collective security. An attack on one is an attack on all. If one is attacked, all defend.

From day one it was clear that it's us versus them out on the streets.

The indoctrination sometimes worked against the training.

One class was finished off with different instructional tactics, such as handcuffing a prisoner, the proper use of a nightstick, or removing a weapon from a suspect. At that time the recruits were also required to box. Not as a sport but to learn how to defend one's self. For the younger recruits like me this was fun. The only problem I really saw with it was no one took it seriously. How were we supposed to bring ourselves to punch people we now considered friends? While this lesson was being taught, a big recruit named Tony Donato grabs my foot, yanks my sneaker off, and lets it fly across the gym. At this point everybody breaks out laughing. Of course I'm trying to just hide my foot sitting there with one sneaker on and the other forty feet away. The instructor wanted to know whose sneaker just flew across his gym. I knew it wouldn't be hard to figure out it was mine. So I man up, confess it's mine, and eventually limp across

```
the gym—as my classmates snickered—to
get the shoe.
```

For the next thirty minutes or so Donato and Eurell worried about what, if any, were the repercussions of flying footwear. At the end of class, the instructor ordered Ken to come see him, making no mention of Donato.

"Hey, I'll go with you," said Donato, "I'll just tell 'em the truth."

Ken Eurell, age twenty, tapped into the deep rivers of New York heritage and uttered words that form the cornerstone of truly lasting relationships: "Why should we both get in trouble? You stay here. I'm going in alone."

"Who threw your shoe?" the instructor asked.

"I don't know," Ken replied.

The instructor pressed the issue.

"How could you not know who took that sneaker off your foot and threw it forty feet across the gym?"

"Well," answered Ken as if he were Leo Gorcey responding to Pat O'Brian in the classic movie, *Angels with Dirty Faces*, "I was paying such close attention to the lesson, I just didn't notice who took it."

The instructor looked closely at Ken Eurell as if attempting to read his very soul. He paused thoughtfully before delivering a prefabricated lecture on department screw-ups that held no threats, blatant nor subtle. He then calmly told Ken to return to his company. No punishment, no reprisals.

Another student may have missed the message, but Ken understood.

```
The instructor was impressed with my
rookie understanding of the Blue Wall of
silence.
```

Self-serving or not, Ken was probably 100 percent correct.

My first cover-up happened before I
ever set foot on the streets. Ultimately
I learned you could get away with things
in the police department. Other than
that, the NYPD academy seemed little
different than high school.

One significant difference was that Ken wasn't much of a drinker in high school. He and his buddies would have some beers, but he wasn't a binge drinker or a falling down drunk. Becoming a cop dramatically accelerated his alcohol consumption.

Once I entered the police academy my
drinking was pushed along to a new level.
Alcohol opened up new social doors for
me, but it also opened a new world of
tension and problems.

The change in Ken's personality was immediately noticeable, especially to his parents. When Ken was drinking, he was a happy guy.

Nothing annoyed me or got on my
nerves, but once I put the bottle down,
my temper flared up. The smallest things
triggered arguments with my parents or
my girlfriend.

There is an old saying, "Get enough clowns together and

sooner or later you're gonna have a circus." It's the same with alcohol-influenced cops. Get enough of them together and you get the clowns and the circus.

## CHAPTER 7. THE BOOZE & THE BLUE

One Friday night all the recruits from our company went out for drinks. We were bar hopping. Nearing the end of the night, at the 007 bar in the city, there were just six of us left. At one point Dan Dorian, my ride, got up and left for the bathroom.

When he returned to our table he had this shit-eating grin. Under his jacket there's the shape of a big square. He had stolen a Heineken mirror from the men's room wall.

My friend Frank Essig, who was in the academy with us, asked, "What the hell are you smiling about Dan?"

"I've got to go now," Dan replied. Then he bolted toward the door and out to the street.

Essig and I sprinted out after him. He was our ride home. When we got outside, there was Dorian hailing a cab. As the cabbie came to a stop, Dorian tried to get into the front seat. We could hear the cabbie yelling.

"Backseat! Backseat!"

Dorian was wild-eyed.

"Fuck you, Gunga Din!" he screamed at the Indian cabbie.

Then Dorian, never politically correct, ran away again.

When we caught up to him we decided to start looking for his car, a big and very old, four-door Cadillac. Dan was so drunk he couldn't remember where he parked it. He was also too drunk to drive, but we couldn't stop him.

"Where the hell are you driving?" Essig asked.

"My bar!" was Dan Dorian's drunken reply as the car lurched into the street.

We were going pretty fast. Then Dan, drunk off his ass, suddenly shouted "Brake check!"

He slammed on the brakes. I flew face first into the back of the front seats. I couldn't help wondering how I got into this situation.

Somehow we arrived, mostly unscathed, at Dorian's neighborhood bar in Queens. His bar is a storefront in the middle of the block. There's one big window with the security gate pulled down. A Dumpster sat on the street outside the window. It was a shithole. We parked. Essig and I sat in the car while Dorian got out and insisted that his friend, the owner, let us come in the place.

Finally the owner agreed, and Dorian gave us the sign that let us know we were okay. He then walked over to the Dumpster and, in full view of the street, zipped down his fly and relieved himself. There was a miniature river flowing down the side of the steel garbage container.

I wanted to be home. But that wasn't

happening. We stepped inside this bar.

"One beer," the owner growled before pulling the plug on the jukebox.

Dorian wasn't up to taking any shit. He plugged it back in and explained how things were going to work.

"I'll be the judge of how many beers we have," he told his friend.

And with that, beer was served.

I began to look around and realized the bar was like something out of a bad movie or TV show. It was dark, dirty, and a downer. Neon signs and mirrors made the place look a little bigger than a hole in the wall it was. Only regulars ever came in here. As my eyes adjusted to the low light, I could see an old guy was passed out with his head down on the bar.

While we're drinking our beers Essig asked another patron, a skinny, greasy guy with shoulder-length hair in his mid-to-late twenties for directions to the restroom. The skinny guy pulls out his dick and pisses on the side of the bar.

"Right here buddy," he slurred.

With that, Essig and I walked out. Dorian followed us. With the help of someone's guardian angel we made it home that night.

None of us needed a guardian angel to finish up our training.

During the last week of the police academy we had to run an obstacle course in a required time in order to pass our physical training requirement. The course included obstacles such as climbing a wall and crawling under a bunch of tables that had been placed end-to-end.

We were all trying to set the academy record, going all out at top speed. One guy, a small wiry guy, actually did beat the record.

Essig, though, got hurt. When it was his turn to run the course he dove at the first set of tables, landed with his palms down and immediately dislocated his shoulder. They took him to the hospital across the street. Even though he was hurt, we couldn't pay much attention. Our testing continued.

An injury in the academy was like the kiss of death. Essig's shoulder could have been real trouble. Afterward, while we were down in the locker room changing, Essig strolled in with his arm in a sling. He explained to us how they popped his shoulder back into place and then removed the sling.

"Look I'm fine," he said, moving his arm in a 360-degree rotation like an airplane propeller.

More like twenty years old, stupid, and indestructible.

Gun and Shield Day came six months after we started in the academy. As official members of the NYPD, we were given a service weapon and a badge and warned that during that first year we would be on probation and could be fired for any reason at all.

Getting through it all was an opportunity to celebrate as we knew with graduation we would be separated and assigned to different spots all over the city.

Several of us went out after the ceremony. It was the first night we could carry weapons—a Smith and Wesson .38 with a four-inch barrel. The gun is a real pain in the ass to keep concealed, especially for a drunk twenty-year-old. And I was toasted that night. My gun was hanging out of my backside.

It probably scared the shit out of Joe Citizen. The bouncer at one place came over and said, "Hey your gun is exposed. I'm going to call the cops."

"We are the cops," I explained.

My friends, who were slightly less drunk than I, got my gun, removed the bullets, and then gave it back. Drunkenly I slurred the words to the Lynyrd Skynyrd hit "Gimme Back My Bullets" as it played on the jukebox.

I was so drunk that a group of the guys dropped me off at a nearby apartment. They went back to celebrate.

Sometime later, one of the guys came back to the apartment alone. He also passed out drunk. Eventually Frank Essig and two other guys were ready to call it a night and they came back, only they couldn't get into the apartment. In my stupor I sort of heard the bell ringing over and over with my name being called, but I was unable to respond in any way at all. Finally the guys passed out drunk against the door in the hallway. In the morning we opened the apartment door and the three of them came falling in like they were the Three Stooges.

That night was my first blackout.

Give the entire city of New York a blackout, such as the one in July of 1977, and there is citywide panic.

It was twenty-five hours in the middle of a mid-June heatwave; ConEdison, the power company for New York, called it an act of God. I guess God is into some strange acts because there were lightning bolts hitting power generators simultaneously in Westchester County and elsewhere. Believe me, what happened next was sheer madness.

## CHAPTER 8. CROOKLYN

When New York blacked out, whole neighborhoods became hunting grounds for depraved thugs, muggers, and thieves. Every facet of life in New York was affected. No power meant no refrigeration, no lights, and in some cases, no gas and no water.

Sure it happened before I became a cop, but everybody who lived in New York then remembers the blackout. Brooklyn went up in flames. Looting and vandalism ran rampant. The cops tried to stop it, and they were overwhelmed. Brooklyn gangsters stole toys, clothes, appliances, and furniture. Much of the looting happened in stores that were fully engulfed in flames. Hundreds were treated in hospitals around the city as people were shot, stabbed, and otherwise injured.

Officers described stationing themselves outside stores and clubbing anyone who tried to flee—even then they couldn't stop the madness. By night's end, officials said 2,000 had been arrested. Several thousand more took their free shit and vanished into the darkness.

One story from that night illustrates how crazy it was—and how stupid some people can be. A looter who took an air conditioner brought it home for his grandmother in hopes she would be comfortable in the heat. When they plugged in it—and it failed to work—rather than attribute the failure to the power outage, the grandmother flew into a rage and tossed the A/C unit out her apartment window. She then demanded her grandson go back into the fray and find a unit that worked.

ConEd officials, who just a week before said the power in New York wouldn't fail in a heatwave, had egg on their face, and politicians demanded answers.

"We've seen our citizens subjected to violence, vandalism, theft, and discomfort, the blackout threatened our safety and seriously impacted our economy," Mayor Abe Beame said. "We've been needlessly subjected to a night of terror in many cities that have been looted and burned. The cost, when finally tallied, will be enormous."

Beame, who piloted the city through its worst financial crisis, laid off a bunch of cops to pay for it. He paid the price he didn't win reelection to a second term.

With Beame gone, New York put itself on a path to reinvention.

Robert J. McGuire, writing in the Fall 1982 edition of *Journal of Criminal Law & Criminology*, described a city where every agency of the criminal justice system was overwhelmed. The jails were full. Most criminals knew that if they were arrested for anything short of murder they would be back on the street plying their trade within hours. Muggers and thieves acted with impunity in the late '70s and early '80s.

McGuire explained how the city planned to deal with its problems by implementing a two-pronged approach.

First, officers and prosecutors were directed to target career criminals. Convicted felons committed the vast majority of felonies, so it made sense to go after them, lock them up, and where possible, throw away the key. In California, the idea was given form with the state's very tough "Three Strikes Law." Felons who committed a third strike—even it was a petty theft—would be sentenced to twenty-five years to life in state prison. Judges were given no discretion to deal with these cases, and jails began to fill as crime rates dropped to historic lows. In 1982 it was McGuire who laid out a philosophy that would come to define US criminal justice for much of the next three decades.

"The central point of this policy is that the longer habitual felons are in prison, the fewer felonies they commit upon innocent citizens in society. The ultimate goal of the program is the strategic reduction of violent crime, over time, through the timely incarceration of persons who, by virtue of their criminal history, will predictably commit robberies or other crimes of violence while at liberty. Collectively, this class of career criminals, though a relatively small percentage of the criminal population, is thought to commit a disproportionately high percentage of violent street crime."[1]

The second tenet explained by McGuire was the practice that would come to be known as "Community Oriented Policing."

"Beyond the critical necessity of building better cases where crimes have already been committed, the problem of how best to deploy patrol resources to deter crime before it happens is the enduring problem for police administrators," he explained. "But crime on the streets of our neighborhoods can be reduced only through a partnership of police and residents.

"The cruelest aspect of urban crime is its devastating and disproportionate impact upon the poor and the minority citizens who are the most vulnerable, emotionally and economically, to the social and personal disruptions of endemic criminal behavior. A preponderance of the major

---

1   http://scholarlycommons.law.northwestern.edu/cgi/viewcontent.
cgi?article=6324&context=jclc

offenses in our cities occur in what we euphemistically call the inner city."[2]

In New York City in 1981, Neighborhood Stabilization Units did community policing. The units were largely staffed with rookies who walked foot beats in various tough neighborhoods. Kenny Eurell was assigned to NSU 14 in the heart of Brooklyn's Bedford-Stuyvesant neighborhood. On the streets they called the little slice of hell "Crooklyn."

His academy buddy Essig got the same assignment.

Bed-Stuy in 1981 was no picnic. Along Fulton Street, down-and-outers warmed themselves by trashcan fires. Fast food joints sold fried chicken at every corner. Clothing vendors hawked their lines on the sidewalk. Drug abuse was rampant, and crime was on the rise. The 650-square block area was a mostly black neighborhood with a population of about 218,000 in 1980. That number had dropped from a high of 328,000 ten years earlier.

Services were deteriorating. Fully three out of ten residents were on welfare, and the median family income was $8,500 a year. By contrast, annual median income in the US in 1980 was well above $16,000.

With poverty came crime. Violent crime rates in Bed-Stuy were well above those of New York as a whole and way out of whack with the rest of the county. Labor statistics showed that 15 percent of Bed-Stuy residents were unemployed. Half of all teens were high school dropouts, and standardized tests indicated that 40 percent of school kids could neither read nor write.

Vital shops on Fulton Street or Nostrand Avenue were shuttered by the dozens. As many as 3,000 homes were vacant or acting as shelter for drug-addled squatters. Oftentimes families stayed until the power, water, and gas were shut off, then they'd move on to the next opportunity.

2   Ibid

Perhaps the best description of Bed-Stuy would be "shithole," but the comparison could be construed by shit as a pejorative. Bed-Stuy was America's worst New York nightmare. Ken knew why he was there.

The new officers were to be patrolling where the crime rate was high. You're to be a visible deterrent. All the rookies were on their best behavior waiting to get off their one-year probation.

At that time NSU 14 covered the 77th, 79th, and 88th precincts. Crime was high in each, but Ken soon learned there wasn't a lot of proactive policing being practiced.

On a weekend shift early in his career Ken and his buddy Essig, both of whom were walking a foot beat, decided to have lunch in the 77th Precinct Annex.

The building is somewhat iconic in Brooklyn. It has a large desk to the left of the lobby door. A few scenes from the film "Serpico" were filmed there. The cops who worked there knew their station as "The Alamo."

In the heart of a down-and-out neighborhood, officers developed an "us-versus-them" mentality that solidified the imaginary Blue Wall that separated the police force from the citizens it was allegedly protecting.

There is a broken window theory of neighborhood policing. The thought behind it stems from a belief that, left unimpaired, a broken window is an invitation to criminals. It says no one cares about this neighborhood, its residents, its businesses, or its character. If anything, Brooklyn was one giant broken window.

If there were any security for its residents, it didn't come from the members of the New York Police Department. It especially didn't come from the collection of 200 or so misfits, drunks, petty criminals, and crooks that inhabited "The Alamo."

Serpico was small-time crap compared to what was going on in Crooklyn. Ken didn't know it at the time, but the Seven Seven was a cesspool of corruption and the center of a racket that, for participating officers, netted huge financial gains. Just like scandals of old, officers in the 77th Precinct were routinely robbing dope dealers, dice games, prostitutes, and the occasional citizen.

Cops involved in the more lucrative shakedowns netted cash that oftentimes tripled their salaries. Many of them justified their behavior with mental gymnastics that implied robbing drug dealers was a more effective method of crime suppression than arrest.

The overcrowding of the jails, overwhelmed prosecutors, and unreliable witnesses added up to a mess on the streets. Let's say Ralph, a street corner drug dealer, gets arrested on Monday morning. More often than not Ralph would be back at the same corner Wednesday afternoon selling crack vials from the same package. Many cops saw their fight against drugs as an uphill battle, often unsupported by higher ups who didn't give a shit about two-bit drug dealers. That's not to say the brass didn't support their street cops in other ways.

Police brutality cases were often shrugged off, and civilian complainers were forced to jump through a series of hoops that discouraged reporting bad cops. Cops who dared take on their colleagues were scorned as "rats." Often their lockers were broken into, or they were gifted with dead rats and ostracized by their colleagues for daring to expose what was happening behind the Blue Wall.

Dope wasn't the only way for cops to make an extra buck. Often before a shift began officers on patrol would confer with each other and determine who would get credit for any arrests that day. More often than not those arrests would come at the end of a shift, which resulted in the accrual of overtime. After all, there is a lot of paperwork to fill out following an arrest.

Often the "arresting" officer would make up the circumstances of the arrest, without actually knowing what happened. Seldom—if ever—were these bogus arrests challenged in court. The cops of the 77th eventually learned it was easier to take a cut of dope or money and let the suspect go with a beating or a warning. For the most part suspects appreciated getting a pass—it was a hell of a lot easier than getting busted and maybe having to do jail or prison time.

Of course the sergeants and lieutenants were in on the game—at least looking the other way especially when few drugs or a small amount of money was vouchered following an arrest.

There were other ways to pull off shit.

If cops in the Seven Seven had a location they wanted to hit, oftentimes the officers would call 911 from the field and report something that required immediate police response to the location. They were literally dropping their own dimes. Internal Affairs investigators and even state prosecutors knew something smelled in the Seven Seven, but the group of bad cops had inside knowledge provided by a union rep who was a sergeant in that very same precinct. That knowledge kept them one step ahead of nosy Internal Affairs investigators.

Anytime investigators got close, the ring leaders shut down their activity until things cooled off. In the early1980s, a ring of corrupt officers in the 77th Precinct, known as the Buddy Boys, were judge, jury, and sometimes executioners.

Ken, still fresh to the force, knew none of that. And, there's no way he would have been let into the circle of corruption until he proved himself. That first weekend afternoon on the job, Ken and Essig just wanted lunch.

We go into the annex lounge and the real cops (as rookies called them) were watching a ballgame. Each veteran had chipped in a dollar for a beer run. Essig and I followed along. We drank and watched the game with the real cops.

When we stood up to go back on patrol, the sergeant began to yell.

"Where are you two going?"

"Back to our post boss," I said. "Lunch is over."

"Sit down!" he barked in a drunken slur. "You get more than two beers for a buck."

The rest of the tour was spent drinking in the lounge. It was a smart move. The veteran officers of the 77th partially accepted Kenny into their fraternity. It opened a window into some of the corruption that was plaguing the unit. One afternoon a group of veterans including William "Junior" Gallagher, now comfortable with Kenny's presence, dropped a dime on a location they wanted to hit and asked him if he wanted to see the fireworks.

Since we had beers with them in the lounge, they trusted us enough and allowed us to tag along.

Soon after getting the go-ahead, the veteran officers started jogging down the street with their nightsticks in hand. Their adrenaline was clearly pumping. A few stores down from the annex itself, they stopped at what looked like a harmless bodega-type grocery store.

62

When we arrived, the veteran officers started to take apart the store piece-by-piece. They even ripped out the heavy Plexiglas cage that protected the store's cash register clerk from armed robberies. We kicked and broke some shelves in order to fit in. The clerk was smacked around and thrown out the front door. The veterans told him to never come back.

"This is how you do the job kid," one veteran said.

The pieces came quickly together. The bodega was a front for drug sales. And the lesson was clear: The way to stop drug sales was to apply a massive amount of force—with or without a warrant.

Ken also learned that the clerk was never arrested for selling drugs. If dope was found at the scene it wasn't confiscated as evidence, and any money that was in the store vanished.

I knew it was a quicker and more effective way of stopping drug sales. I also knew that was crossing the line between cop and criminal. I just thought that's how things were done in the NYPD.

Not all the veterans and training officers were cynical burn-outs. But there were plenty of bad apples—and the 77th was ripe for a corruption scandal that would rock the NYPD in just a few years.

A couple of cops in the 77th, Brian O'Regan and Henry Winter, both Buddy Boys, perfected the art of robbing dope dealers. O'Regan, Winter, and eleven other officers in the precinct would be nabbed in a scandal that rocked NYPD from top to bottom. By then Kenny would be long gone and have faint—if any—memories of the duo and their cohorts.

# CHAPTER 9. LAND OF FUCK

Adam Diaz remembers East New York of the early 1980s as a crime-infested and dangerous place. Not a location where a guy would spend much time standing still, that's for sure. A moving target is much harder to hit.

Known as "Blondie," Diaz barely weighed one hundred pounds. He had no problem defending himself but carried a black .45 in his waistband "just-in-case." He moved around a lot. Sometimes he'd be in Washington Heights, sometimes Queens. Other times you might catch Adam and his posse on the dance floor of a smoking hot Miami disco. For weeks at a time he'd disappear on trips to Colombia and conduct his business.

Like Tony Montana, his fictional counterpart in the 1983 film *Scarface*, Adam Diaz, with his shock of reddish-blond hair, had a lot of swagger. He was fearless and tough when he needed to be, but had a kind and gentle side that would surface from time to time. Diaz had a smile that would disarm a skeptical detective and a scowl that would scare the toughest of street thugs.

When Adam was in New York you might find him in one of his three grocery stores, otherwise Diaz was challenging traffic laws and traffic jams zipping around on one of his two motorcycles—red and black "Ninja 1000s."

In his mid-twenties, Diaz was one of the city's top coke dealers. Just fifteen when he came to the US from the Dominican Republic, Diaz started his career as teen on a street corner dealing packages for his brother. He soon proved he was good enough at moving coke to get a meeting with the very elusive Nicky Barnes, a gangster whom New

York scribes knew as "Mr. Untouchable."

New York writers and reporters had Barnes pegged. Although he was flashy and easy to spot, Barnes was slippery. He watched his back around the NYPD and only got busted after the DEA slipped an undercover informant into his organization. Barnes dealt heroin but wasn't averse to making a buck or two on cocaine—and the late 1970s was a time when cocaine use was on the rise. Why not hook up with a couple of streetwise Dominicans for a deal now and then?

By the time Nicky had gone away, Adam commanded his own organization and regularly moved kilos of coke from the Columbian cartel into Washington Heights, the Lower East Side, East New York, and Queens. But he was hard to pin down.

"How the fuck I never got caught, I'll never figure it out," Diaz said. "Maybe with the gun hanging out of my backside the cops thought I was a cop. Maybe it was because I looked white? I'm lucky that's for sure."

By the time he was nineteen, Diaz was living the *Lifestyles of the Rich and Famous*.

"I had a lot of cars. I loved Porsches and Ferraris, and I always had the best sound system installed."

Diaz lived life on the edge, taking chances whenever they arose. He would get his bikes up to top speed and weave in and out of traffic in the Holland Tunnel or on the George Washington Bridge. When he was carrying a load of drugs or cash, Adam used one of his Porsches—preferably the candy red 911. It was his favorite, and he kept it in immaculate condition.

"If I was in a nice neighborhood, people don't care, but in East New York, I thought the cops might say 'I'm going after that kid. If he's not a Rockefeller, then he's doing something illegal.'

"They never did."

It would be difficult to describe Brooklyn's 75th Precinct during the early 1980s. No sensible comparison exists. There was (and is) nothing like it. It was a war zone. Brutality, murder, robbery, and theft ruled the streets. Children grew up quick; parents succumbed to addiction or fled with their families to suburbia.

"Very bad. Very bad," Diaz recalled. "They were shooting all the time. I picked up a couple of guys off the street in East New York. Back then you had to pick people up off the street to take them to the hospital, or else they would die before the police or an ambulance even arrived.

"They tried to kill me a couple of times."

It was an ugly time and a dangerous place for anyone. Diaz's friends were dropping left and right. A welterweight boxer Diaz knew, Lindel Gonzalez, left the ring when he was injured in a violent altercation—OK, it was a shooting.

"I had my Mercedes registered to him," Diaz said, noting that it was a good way to hide income from prying IRS and state tax officials.

As for Lindel?

"He left boxing when he got shot. He was a nice kid, but he got all fucked up. He took forty bullets. He's in a wheelchair now. Can't walk. Shit happened like that every day."

While the shit was going down in Adam's world, rookies Ken Eurell and Frank Essig were learning what it meant to be cops in that environment. Having gone through the academy and field training together, it's no surprise that fellow officers thought the two young men were connected at the hip. If one was at a crime scene or an incident, the other wouldn't be far behind.

When our time in the NSU was up, Essig

and I got sent to the 75th Precinct
which is at 1000 Sutter Avenue in the
East New York section of Brooklyn.

As a team Ken and Essig couldn't wait to get to work as
real cops.

Essig and I decided to stop by the
75th Precinct a day earlier than we were
assigned to report. We wanted to beat
the incoming crowd of rookies to the
limited number of available lockers.
When we arrived we flashed our tins (what
cops call badges) at the gate because we
were in civilian clothing.
"We're assigned to start here
tomorrow."
One of the veterans shouted at us.
"Welcome to the Land of Fuck!"

Ken's first patrol was on the very busy and always
eventful midnight shift. His partner checked out a car from
the motor pool and drove straight up to Highland Park, on
the north end of the precinct near Queens. They went deep
inside the park and stopped.

Then and there Ken learned the fine art of "cooping"—
napping on the job. Before Ken's fat and out-of-shape new
partner fell asleep he had some questions.

"You play ball?"

"Sure do."

"Great. We need some young blood ..."

Pretty soon the old-timer was curled up in his patrol
car seat and snoring. The uneventful shift ended with a
complimentary breakfast at a coffee shop closer to the

precinct house.

Ken's next partner was more engaged with the neighborhood. He lived there. Ken couldn't understand why anyone would want to live anywhere in East New York. Even though his new partner was frequently late for work, the supervisors usually gave him a pass. Each morning the excuse was similar.

"You know boss, I just got to get that last piece of pussy before I come in."

Laughter would ensue and the workday would begin.

Every job that we went to—no matter what it was for, a dispute, robbery, car accident, anything—he always knew someone at the scene. Just about everyone invited us out to drinks or for dinner. For the most part we shied away from making arrests unless we absolutely had to do it.

Even though the precinct was a hot crime area there were few reasons to actually pick up a collar—and none of them had to do with crime suppression.

There were really only two reasons to make an arrest. You make arrests for overtime or to get yourself noticed for a unit transfer. In a jam there was always someone willing to take an arrest if you didn't want to. My new partner was burned out on the job and didn't want the additional work. I went with the flow.

Every now and then police work had to be done. Ken, an auto buff, liked to help find stolen cars. He was good at it, but a lot of times his penchant for chasing hot wheels got Ken in trouble. If he was going to get along with his fellow officers, Ken had to learn the rules. Sometimes those rules meant cops didn't chase every stolen car in Brooklyn. Sometimes Ken couldn't contain himself.

> I was in the station house and overheard a civilian reporting his brand new black Trans Am stolen. I probably listened more intently than I would have for the simple reason it involved a car.

During their shift that evening Ken and his partner parked their patrol car outside a gas station while the owner closed up shop. Call it a courtesy. The shop owner would have cash on hand and would be a likely target for a rip-off or a mugging.

While the cops were watching the store, a black Trans Am appeared on the street.

Ken shouted, "Hey, there goes that stolen car!"

> I called in the plate, but the dispatcher didn't have it listed as stolen. Word hadn't got that far. Even so we hit the lights and pulled the driver over and made an arrest. We recovered the car before the owner even got home. The owner was pretty happy with us.

Another time Ken helped out a school teacher. She was the sister of a fellow cop who always parked her ride near the elementary school at the corner of Pennsylvania and Pitkin.

Ken's eye for cars made him a pro at spotting pinched cars.

> She had a white Buick Skylark that I
> always noticed in the neighborhood. One
> day I see the car about a mile from the
> school. I immediately recognized it, and
> when I saw she wasn't driving it, I knew
> it was stolen.

Ken sat on the car and called the woman's father to come and pick it up. That way he saved the car and prevented her from getting hit with towing and impound fees—always a huge hit that follows the recovery of a stolen car.

> When her dad picked up the car he
> offered me money as a thank you for taking
> the time to recover the car and wait on
> it. I refused. I thought it would be
> corruption.

Pretty soon, Ken and Frank were paired up in a patrol car. After hours the men played on the precinct's softball team. It helped them fit in with the senior officers. Eventually they got to participate in other extracurricular activities that were only open to cops who could be trusted.

At one retirement party the rookies stood side-by-side with veterans and brass and watched with amusement as three strippers took care of the guest of honor.

> We soon began to practically live
> in the precinct. If we didn't know the
> victim or the perpetrators we would know
> people standing around near the scene of
> a crime.

Ken and Frank were beginning to fit in while learning the dos and don'ts of being a cop. They also learned what it meant to be valued members of the precinct softball team.

One morning around three, officers received a radio call claiming there was a man with a gun in the neighborhood. The dispatch went to a member of the softball team who decided to take his time getting to the scene in hopes it would give the perp plenty of time to get away.

As a result Ken and Frank arrived first.

As we drove up, a suspect fitting the description is walking down the middle of the street. Frank and I jump out of the patrol car, pull our guns, and in perfect academy banter shout, "Police. Don't move!"

Just as Frank and Ken disarmed the man, who was carrying a fully loaded semi-automatic pistol, their teammate arrived on scene.

"What the hell are you guys doing? You have to play softball in the morning!" The angry cop pulled his partner out of their patrol car and exclaimed, "He's taking the collar. You guys need your rest."

That rookie season also gave Ken a glimpse of the danger of the job and the brutality that often accompanies a close call.

It all began with the sort of radio call that no cop wants to hear.

"Ten-thirteen! Ten-thirteen! Officer down!"

We're literally a block away from the location. We show up, jump out, and help the shot officer and his partner into the car, while other crime cops are dragging the cuffed perp to their unmarked car. We race off to Baptist Medical Center on Linden Boulevard. We have a great relationship with the staff there, and they are waiting for us in the parking lot as we roll up.

As we're headed to the hospital, we learn how our buddy got shot. He was attempting to make an arrest, and the subject, a teenager, was down on the ground.

Suddenly the kid comes out with a gun from behind his back. He shoots up at the cop who takes it in his upper thigh. The bullet traveled upward and back, lodging in the anti-crime officer's buttocks.

We got him to the hospital, gave statements to the detectives, and returned to the station house.

A trail of blood led from the parking lot, through the back doors, past the front desk, and up the front stairwell to the anti-crime office. The kid behind the shooting was cuffed and curled up in the fetal position on the floor of the office. Blood pooled on the floor.

In those days cops didn't think twice about "tuning up" a piece-of-shit perp that well deserved it. Street justice was the rule, not the exception, and Frank was going to mete out some punishment to the bloodied asshole.

He walks up to the perp and rears back

and kicks him in the stomach. That sent
a message: Don't fuck with us.

It didn't take long for Ken to get some other knowledge that would help him better understand the Seven Five—116 Williams Avenue.

Formerly the site of PS 63, the three-story brick building at Liberty and Williams had been declared surplus in 1980 and converted into a men's shelter by the city's board of health. Located in a mostly industrial neighborhood, 116 Williams was the source of numerous calls for service. Invariably the homeless residents of the location frequently assaulted each other or the security guards who worked at the shelter. It was a place the cops tried to avoid as much as possible.

As you pulled up in front of the
building the wave of body odor wafting
out the front doors was so strong it
was stomach turning. Being inside the
building was like being in a scene from
The Walking Dead.

Hairbags—the senior officers in the squad—knew to avoid calls for service from the location. If they heard something dispatched to the location, old-timers would hold off an immediate response in hopes that they could take advantage of the naivety of those who were new to the precinct.

It was definitely a low priority
location, regardless of the job coming
over.

It wasn't just cops who were leery of the shelter. UPS

drivers would get ripped off routinely at the location. It got to be a running joke in their dispatch terminals that 116 Williams was a not only a dead end for the dregs of society, it was the end of any package that got within a block.

Two months after they were placed in the same patrol car, Ken and Essig were abruptly separated by a new sergeant who was intent on enforcing every one of NYPD's arcane department rules. The new sergeant harassed everyone in the 75th Precinct about mundane and petty bullshit. Even the veterans were getting docked for all sorts of rule violations. It was if the new sergeant was trying to prove something. Clearly he didn't get the memo about the Seven Five being the Land of Fuck.

```
    Not only that, this sergeant kept
following Essig and me from job to job
making sure our jackets were on, our
ties were done, and our sleeves were
buttoned.
```

Eventually Ken and the officious sergeant had words over the condition of Ken's uniform. Ken was told to stay after work, and it rankled him. But he met with his superior in the precinct's briefing room in front of several other officers who were returning from duty or headed out to the field.

"He starts yelling at the top of his lungs and pointing his finger at me like he's a parent scolding a small child."

Ken suddenly "got it." The boss was just another bully, and Big Jim told Ken how you deal with bullies.

"I can hear you fine without you jabbing your finger at me," Ken shot back, landing a solid and unexpected verbal blow.

"I'll point my finger wherever I want," the boss said, raising the stakes and his voice.

Ken didn't raise his voice. He didn't need to, not with a delivery cold enough to freeze concrete and a tone that resonated from a deep core of steely toughness

"Do it again," promised Ken evenly, "and I'll break it off and shove it up your ass."

Ken turned on his heel, as if punctuating a display of absolute power and authority, and walked calmly out of the room.

Jaws dropped with incredulity and honest-to-God respect for Ken Eurell. That "I take no shit" demonstration accomplished several import things—no one ever jabbed their finger at him again, his reputation as a boss-fighter was cinched beyond doubt, and Officer Michael Dowd, who watched the confrontation in rapt attention, decided he needed to work with this Kenny Eurell guy.

He'd have to wait. Two days after the finger-pointing party in the day room, Ken packed up his locker and began work in the 88th Precinct. The incident made it impossible for Ken to stay in the Seven Five and he was transferred to the Eight Eight at the foot of the Brooklyn Bridge.

One cop who watched Ken go was New York Police Officer Henry "Chickie" Guevara. He had arrived in the Seven Five right after Ken, straight out of his NSU assignment in the 113th Precinct on Jamaica Avenue Queens.

Before he was a real police, Chickie was a transit officer. The subways weren't exactly a danger free zone, and Chickie saw things right out of a horror movie.

"If you said you weren't scared, you were full of shit," said Guevara. "We were issued radios that were the size of a shoe box. But since most of the city's transit system is underground, the radios mostly didn't work. If you needed back-up, forget it. There was no calling the cavalry; there was no calling anyone."

Guevara's assignment was on the midnight shift. He'd

ride the N line from Coney Island to Manhattan and back again.

"You wanna know how bad it was? I'll tell you how bad it was."

# CHAPTER 10. CHICKIE

"You had to be able to handle a lot of shit," recalled Chickie, who speaks with the thick and characteristic accent of a Queens native. "There'd be people on the train who were drunk or high; there were homeless sleeping on the train. You have to realize how horrific it was. Then these fucks would jump out in front of a train to kill themselves. I don't understand how it's a good suicide to get run over by a train. You'd see their bodies mangled or folded to torn apart. I was glad to get out of there."

From transit Guevara went to Queens. Although he didn't know it, he was destined to wind up in Brooklyn. He wanted to be anywhere else.

"You wanted to go to certain precincts. Women see a guy in uniform, it's like Spanish Fly for them. A uniform makes women horny," Guevara said. "We all wanted to go to where the women were. Upper East Side would be good. I like Asians. I was hoping I'd get sent to Chinatown. Everybody had a place they wanted to go."

Getting an assignment you really wanted in the NYPD came down to one thing—a hook. Guevara and Kenny described a hook as someone in the department who acted as a mentor and helped guide the careers of young officers.

"I didn't have a hook," Guevara said. "I got sent to the Seven Five."

Guevara's field training officer, a hairbag who didn't have much pull in the department, nonetheless promised to smooth the transition.

"Listen Chickie, I'm going to call over there to some guys I know and make sure you get on the best squad,"

Guevara's mentor promised. "No midnights, and you'll get into a car as soon as possible.'"

The best squad in any precinct was the one officers referred to as the "Holiday Squad." For the most part, cops in the Holiday Squad worked a straight nine to five and the occasional swing shift. No midnights.

"I got paired up with an Irish cop, and we hit it off pretty well," Guevara said.

Chickie's first day on the job typified life in the Seven Five. He reported to work at 3:30 p.m. and at 4:00 p.m. was standing out in front of a grocery store examining a dead body.

"It was an Arab dude," Guevara said. "He was standing in front of a bodega. The shot that took him out went through his head, through the front door of the bodega, through the glass door of the beer cooler, and through two cans of beer before it ran out of juice.

"So I'm working that case, and I get back on the street four or five hours later and we catch another. This time it's a kid. He's laid out on the stoop. Not shot in the head. There wasn't even a lot of blood. He was wearing a dark shirt so there was no real contrast. The hairbag that was with me lifted up his shirt."

"See these tiny little holes? That's where he got shot."

Guevara soaked it up.

"Got a forensic lesson that day too, I guess."

Not much later, April 15, 1984, to be exact, Guevara was on duty and assigned to the scene of a mass shooting that would become known as "The Palm Sunday Massacre." Ten people—three adults, a teenager, and six children—were shot to death execution-style in a cramped first floor apartment on Liberty Avenue in the heart of East New York.

Carmine Rossi, a neighbor who made the gruesome discovery, told reporters, "Bodies were all over the place."

Three of the victims were huddled together in an oversized orange arm chair. The television was on. An infant who survived the ordeal wailed on the floor and was rescued by Rossi and eventually adopted by one of the New York Police officers who were dispatched to the grisly and incomprehensible scene.

"They were sitting up," Rossi said, describing the bloody massacre. "It looked like a wax museum, like dummies."

Eventually police arrested a man identified as Christopher Thomas, thirty-five, from the Bronx. He was high on crack when he committed the murders. Jurors in his trial found Thomas guilty on ten counts of manslaughter and one count of possessing a dangerous weapon.

Jurors said they settled on manslaughter instead of murder because Thomas was suffering from the emotional distress of being under the influence of cocaine.

"He'd been freebasing for two years," one juror remarked. "That would make anybody emotionally disturbed."

The bodies piled up in the Seven Five. If the cops weren't at a murder scene they were cleaning up after a suicide.

"We had people jumping off buildings on the south end of the precinct all the time," Guevara said.

The constant horror of the job drew the cops closer to one another. Ken and Chickie both said it explained the existence of the Blue Wall. It bound them together and separated them from the unwashed masses of citizens who needed their help. It was also the glue that kept cops from ratting each other out.

The wall formed naturally. Policing the Seven Five was a decidedly "us versus them" venture.

A call to a housing project meant getting showered by a ghetto ticker tape parade. The rain of shit included a special mix of glass bottles, spit, and whatever else could be hurled or tossed from above. Most of the time it was harmless, but the constant assault on officers had elements of danger as well.

Guevara was sleeping off a hangover in a patrol car one afternoon shift when a cinderblock was tossed off a ten-story building and connected with the windshield. When it hit, the cement building block and tempered-glass windshield of the patrol car exploded in unison like a cannon shot. Glass shattered, rock splintered, and Chickie was roused from his uncomfortable and sweaty post-drunk snooze.

"I wake up, and I can't see anything," he said. "My partner knew what happened. He also knew we were never going to catch the kid who did it."

Working in the constantly brutal and unforgiving Seven Five darkened Guevara's outlook on life in general, and he began to see stark contrasts between himself, his buddies, and their surroundings.

"Eventually the job gets to you. You get to the point where you are saying, 'What the fuck am I doing here?'" Guevara said. "Eventually, you don't even like cops, but you realize you can't do it by yourself, and if you are screaming into the radio for help you want your brothers to be there for you."

Cops in the Seven Five knew they were different. They weren't like the pretty boy officers with the well-pressed uniforms, gleaming badges, and perfectly pointed hats lining a parade route in Manhattan. There was no way the perfect cops would be able to handle a real event like the annual West Indian Day Parade that brings half-naked carnival girls and crazily high Rastafarians to the streets for an annual Labor Day orgy that typically sputters way out-of-control and more often than not turns violent and ugly.

But it wasn't all shit. Every day on the job also held opportunity. In the ghetto, business owners worried constantly about getting robbed. Those Plexiglas dividers that separated clerks from violent, potential robbers didn't just pop up in liquor stores. They were in take-out Chinese restaurants, grocery stores, and just about anywhere else where cash talks and the guy asking for credit has a FICO score approaching zero and is probably already deep into the numbers runners, dope dealers, and loan sharks.

Chickie and his buddies saw themselves as the ghetto's Plexiglas. They expected to be rewarded for their service. It was a strictly cash business.

The reality was this: Cops kept things from turning into *Lord of the Flies*. Business owners were grateful for their presence. In the Seven Five in the 1980s nothing was out of a cop's reach. Restaurant owners fed their protectors, grocery stores turned over packs of cigarettes, and hookers gave head. That's how it worked. One good turn deserved another. You scratch my back, I'll scratch yours.

"Go ahead officer, grab a six-pack from the cooler. We're behind you 100 percent."

A free meal resulted in a nice tip and a verbal note to your buddies in the precinct house that a certain business owner was "on the arm" or "on the cuff." Once a cop and a business owner had a relationship, it was looked at as an inviolable contract.

"I never paid for flowers. I never paid for beer. I never bought a meal. I never reached for my wallet to pay for a pack of cigarettes. Never bought my own drugs. Never paid for anything," Guevara said.

A cop's contacts were that cop's contracts. That's how it worked. You never took from another cop's contacts unless you asked first.

"You never want to bend a guy over too much," Guevara said.

If a business owner on the arm needed an escort to the bank, he'd get one. No questions asked.

After the murders and the suicides and the free meals, the rest of police work was bullshit. No one wanted to arrest a guy carrying three nickel bags—about $15 worth of stepped on shit. A collar like that and you'd be down at Central Booking for eight or more hours just to get the perp checked in. And that sucked. You let things go.

It was learned behavior because just about every police officer goes to the job with a dream of doing the right thing.

At first the cop arrested the guy with the three nickel bags. The cop graduated into tossing the bags down the sewer and letting the perp go with an understanding that escaping justice meant the perp had entered into a bargain with the police. He now owed them a favor.

Pretty soon the cop grabbed the three nickel bags and passed them off to a brother-in-law at a cut rate. You'd get fifteen bags in a score, tell the brother-in-law to pay for ten, and keep the other five.

Pretty soon you'd catch the eye of other cops who knew what was going on. Crack cocaine was everywhere and so was the money it generated. No way to ignore it.

Back in the 1970s, the Knapp Commission, which investigated charges that arose out of the Frank Serpico case, identified two kinds of corrupt cops—meat-eaters and grass-eaters.

"Meat-eaters ... aggressively misuse their police powers for personal gain. The grass-eaters simply accept the payoffs that the happenstances of police work throw their way."

Eventually meat-eaters devoured the grass-eaters. There was no other possible outcome. Chickie said the slide from herbivore to carnivore was unavoidable in the Seven Five, and anyone who was close to get a whiff could smell the corruption.

Ghetto dwellers knew what was up with the police. Everybody outside the ghetto had their heads up their asses.

Cops working the Seven Five precinct eventually gravitated toward the cops that could be trusted—cops who knew how to act. Guevara trusted Mike Dowd, a guy who knew every one of the five-square miles that made up New York's 75th Precinct.

Dowd's reputation preceded him. Those who knew the real Mike Dowd knew he defined the role of a meat-eater in the NYPD. He knew the players, the angles, the odds, and the score. He was a master manipulator and had the top-notch ability to read a situation and understand the larger implications of his actions in any environment. If Dowd was a baseball player he'd be Pete Rose. If he was a politician he'd be Richard Nixon, and if he was a celebrity he'd be MC Hammer or Milli Vanilli or some combination of the two. He was that good and possessed that sort of charisma and charm.

Dowd left an impression in every room he entered. Most times when he removed himself from the room, Dowd's larger-than-life personality left ripples in his wake like a stone thrown into a still pond. Chickie learned that in the Seven Five Dowd was a force to be reckoned with—eventually.

"They say once you take that first hit of crack you're hooked. It's the same way with a big score, when you get your first one—a substantial amount of cash—you can't stop."

The six-foot-two Mikey D, cackled his high-pitched laugh, smiled his gap-toothed grin, and led Chickie by the hand from the precinct house to his first score.

Dowd, known to wear expensive leather and drive fast cars, wasn't simply flamboyant. He was over the top. He snorted coke, drank on duty, and most times when he was wearing the blue, he hung out with unsavory thugs in neighborhood bodegas that were often frequented by notorious mobsters.

A dark-haired, sharp-nosed guy with a cleft chin and an advancing jowl, Dowd's line-creased forehead and slowly receding hairline took some attention away from his shifty coke and booze-addled eyes. Non-New Yorkers would instantly recognize that Dowd spoke in a dialect on the spectrum somewhere between Joe Pesci and Robert DeNiro. New Yorkers knew he spoke like everyone else in Brooklyn. Admittedly dangerous to anyone who might cross him, Dowd used his badge to reap profit from all manner of criminal activity patrolling the mean streets of Brooklyn. Although they were never partners, Dowd taught Chickie the ropes.

Perhaps not too surprisingly Dowd's criminal career nearly began the first day he strapped on a utility belt and service revolver. One of his early scores involved pinching a half key of blow from a crime scene then turning around to sell it for $14,000—nearly half a year's salary for a NYPD cop in the early '80s.

In Dowd's Brooklyn there were good cops and bad cops. And, early on in his career, Dowd developed his own definition of those he befriended. In Dowd's world a "good cop" was a corrupt cop. A brother officer who would look the other way when his partner committed theft, beat the shit out of a suspect, or boozed or did drugs on the job.

The opposite of a "good cop" was a "bad cop"—a cop who wouldn't tolerate misbehavior and might even report it to NYPD superiors.

Dowd wanted to prove early on he was "good." He was intent on becoming a meat-eater. The first opportunity came during a routine drug bust in the projects.

"I noticed a table filled with drugs. Some other officers arrive at the scene. I was a young cop, so they took over the scene and they were in their undercover units, and it wasn't really their job, but they took over. Out of frustration,

I remember reaching into a box full of cocaine and taking out two big handfuls and putting them into my pocket and walking out. I had gotten a new partner at the time, and I had to prove to him that I was good."

Soon Dowd graduated to raiding dealers' stashes. He scored dope, money, and guns as often as five times a day—frequently pocketing an extra $200 in cash per shift. During the holidays, Dowd's take could run as high as $500 a day. Dowd's meat-eating soon proved to be more profitable than it ever had been for corrupt New York cops.

"He's one of those guys who could have been a great cop, but he got off on being a crook," Ken said.

Growing more experienced in law enforcement, Dowd also climbed the criminal ladder. As he learned about the coke trade in Brooklyn and identified the players, Dowd matched buyers and sellers. Soon he was working for dealers and pushers, protecting their stashes, and riding shotgun during deliveries.

Dowd constantly justified his crimes by explaining that good cops had to do bad things.

"The original reason a lot of things are done is not to be so corrupt. In the beginning you start out saying, you know, you're angry that the drug dealers basically run the street and you're angry that you have no dent into what they are doing. So in the beginning you start, well, what the heck? If we arrest them, we get a complaint from our sergeant or (commanding officer). 'What did you do? You took two crack vials off the street? You cost the city sixteen hours of overtime. What's going on here?' This is how it begins, and this is how it begins for us."

Dowd also made a pretty good amount of cash ripping off dead bodies and rolling drunks he encountered on his beat. Dowd once went into a church at the heart of a poor neighborhood and stole ten-pound blocks of government cheese intended for Brooklyn's down-on-their-luck. When he was broke, Dowd pulled over drunks, forced them to empty their wallets, and turned them loose. No one complained. Turning over your cash to a crooked cop was far better than spending the night in the drunk tank of the infamous New York City Tombs.

Like Joseph Wambaugh's *The Choirboys,* Dowd's crew met nightly at a sewage treatment plant in a lonely and quiet area of the Seven Five someone humorously dubbed "The Pool"—as in cesspool. Guevara described its location, off of Flatland Avenue, as the asshole of the precinct. Among the weeds at The Pool, Dowd's buddies would swap stories, pass prostitutes among each other, snort coke, and drink beer. Many nights The Pool would erupt in gunfire as Dowd and his buddies fired their guns into the air or took target practice.

On the streets Dowd maintained order with threats. He told his victims that if they reported his misconduct he'd find them and beat some sense into them.

Beatings were commonplace and sometimes necessary. Residents of the ghetto, known by the cops as "hamsters," needed to be kept in line.

"Plenty of times a guy walks up to you and says, 'If you didn't have that gun and badge, I'd beat the shit out of you," Chickie said. "We'd take that guy, drive him down to the weeds, take off the badge and the gun-belt, and go at it. Half the time the guy wouldn't want to get out of the car. They'd be holding on for dear life. Needless to say they always lost. You wouldn't want to have that guy go back home and say, 'I duked it out with the cops and won.' You'd get no respect."

## CHAPTER 11. BROOKLYN BRIDGE

While Dowd was busy forming his crew, Ken adjusted to his new role in the Eight Eight but longed to return to East New York.

A far cry from the fast-paced Seven Five, the 88th Precinct is primarily residential. Most of its industry lies within the Brooklyn Navy Yard. Ken wanted to return to the action, and he wanted to be with officers he knew and trusted. Upon arriving, Ken put in for a transfer back to East New York.

About the only real excitement in the 88th came from the installation of a statue titled "Don't Jump, Fly" at Fort Greene Park. Intended by its artist as a piece that would discourage suicide, the statue instead prompted an avalanche of calls for help to the Police Department. That's probably because the eight-foot-tall statue was dangling from a railing on the 148-foot-tall Prison Ship Martyrs Monument.

Cops were constantly responding to 911 calls about the alleged jumper.

"There's some new officers around, and maybe they aren't used to it," Lt. Charles Coleman told Cathy Burke, a reporter with United Press International. "A lot of officers don't understand art. Most of the people in the community are aware of it. But at night, I could see how you could mistake it for a rather tall person."

Eventually the statue was removed. Calls for help in the Eight Eight began to take on a more routine flavor, and Ken soon came to realize that being an officer in the 88th had its advantages.

I was playing on the 88th Precinct

88

softball team now and had a motorcycle—
my first street bike.

I was sexually involved with two of
the female officers in the precinct as
well as dating a few other women from my
home area.

On a particularly slow midnight tour
during my first month, I was working with
a young female rookie. We were sitting
in the patrol car parked in a deserted
location. I was enjoying a cup of coffee
and listening to the radio for calls.
My female partner started reading from
Penthouse Forum, the small adult magazine
with erotic letters from readers.

"Hey, listen to this," she said.

It was a letter about oral sex. Here
I am, no girlfriend and this attractive
21-year-old is trying to turn me on by
reading Penthouse Forum letters in the
middle of the night. Let's just say I
actually enjoyed being at work. It was
far less stressful.

On May 24, 1983, I was fortunate to
be assigned the detail to work the one
hundredth anniversary for the Brooklyn
Bridge. All day long people were partying
on the walkway of one of the most famous
bridges in the world. I gladly accepted
drinks as they were offered throughout
the day. I probably had my picture taken
fifty times by people wanting their photo
with one of New York's Finest drinking a
frosty Heineken. At the end of my tour
I hit a local bar with some celebratory

```
locals. I felt as though the 88th Precinct
could be my new home.
```

New York's celebration turned out to be short-lived.

In '83, crack cocaine use spread in numbers that could only be described as epidemic. Former cops and prosecutors characterized Brooklyn's neighborhoods, especially Brownsville, Crown Heights, and East New York, as war zones. All had been hollowed out by crack cocaine.

Meanwhile, trouble was brewing in the 77th Precinct, where Ken's career as a cop began.

Dirty beat cops, known as the "Buddy Boys," were stealing cash and drugs wherever they could get their hands on it. The men, led by Officer Henry Winter, had become a force of their own in the inner city. They alone decided who got arrested, who got a pass, and who got a beat down in a dark alley for contempt of cop.

Winter and other members of the group, including Officer Brian O'Regan, acted with impunity. O'Regan's conduct was especially troubling. Described as a pea-brained weirdo who got off on being a supplicant to Winter and a crooked group of NYPD superiors.

At first, the Buddy Boys only took small amounts of cash. Before long O'Regan and Winter and members of their crew were selling cocaine and guns on the street. Twice they broke into a drug house and sold dope to customers as they arrived, pocketing the cash. In between it all, the Buddy Boys got their daily adrenaline rush answering calls for robberies and rapes. The Buddy Boy's leader, William "Junior" Gallagher, had been partners with Ken's field training officer and led an afternoon raid on a bodega when Ken was training in the Seven Seven.

Similar scams developed in other parts of the city. None of it was exposed. Cops were crooks all over. It wasn't just

Brooklyn that saw the infusion of cocaine money leading to massive corruption schemes. Corruption was happening in Washington Heights, Queens, the Bronx, Far Rockaway, and even sleepy Staten Island.

Why didn't anyone say something? If you were in a precinct house back then you'd know the answer. For the most part the Blue Wall prevented honest cops from ratting on their less-than-honest colleagues.

Take NYPD Officer Bernard Cawley. Assigned to the Bronx's 48th Precinct, Cawley was busy earning his moniker "The Mechanic."

How was he given the nickname?

It was because Cawley was adept at tuning up skels, which is police jargon for beating the shit out of citizens, who didn't necessarily deserve it.

"We just beat people up in general," Cawley said. "If they're on the street, hanging around drug locations. Just—it was a show of force. The sergeant encouraged it, because he pretty much—he rewarded the three guys that were into it: the two other officers and myself. He would reward us: Instead of putting us on foot posts in the winter or something like that, we would drive around in a car with him or the other detectives."

Cawley said tune-ups were a regular part of his job, starting from day one, when he and other officers raided a suspected Bronx drug dealer's hideout.

"They told us, they said, 'Listen we're going over to this building.' … And they said, 'Pretty much everybody in that building, either they're drug dealers or they belong to a motorcycle gang.' They said, 'When we get there, who's ever hanging out they have no right hanging out at this hour of the night.' They said, 'When you go up there just start hitting people.'

"So we start driving over to Davidson and 176th Street;

we came on the block in all different directions. We got out of the car. And as soon as we got out of the police car, the seven cars, we just started beating people. We went into the building, who was ever in the building got beat. A lady was coming down the stairs with a big radio in her hand. They smashed the radio with a nightstick. They threw her down a flight of stairs. It was just anybody who was in that building or right in front of the building got beat that night."

Word got around. In the Seven Five, Officer Mike Dowd was putting together a crew of cops he could trust to beat, rob, and intimidate residents of the precinct. He was certain that much of the work could be done with impunity.

Dowd was twenty when he joined the NYPD in 1982. Within weeks of being put on the streets he was on the take—scoring money, food, and favors where he could get them. Dowd was assigned to the 75th Precinct in 1983 and soon formed a crew that included Chickie Guevara and others. The group was robbing drug dealers typically scoring $500 a week each.

In the 30th Precinct, officers were perfecting many similar schemes. The unit would be eventually known as "The Dirty 30."

Although the shit was going down all over New York, the 88th Precinct remained relatively calm while Ken was there.

Ken not only joined the softball team in his new precinct, He also took to hanging out at the Rail Road Inn in Valley Stream, a suburb just outside of Queens. A red-brick building with peeling whitewashed wood siding and a colorful four-car steam train model painted above the door, the Rail Road Inn lay beneath the Long Island Railroad on South Franklin Avenue. In the mid-1980s, the dive was a popular spot for young adults who popped in to hear DJs spinning anything from Madonna to Billy Idol.

It didn't matter if the tune was Weather Girls singing "It's Raining Men" or the Romantics belting out "What I Like About You," more often than not the dance floor was jumping.

A group of girls in the Rail Road Inn had a special dance they'd perform. The dance, described as a Texas two-step with way more rhythm and a lot more hip shaking was made up by the girls, but the men paid attention.

Leading the charge was Dori Albert, who would soon catch Ken's eye.

Dori, working for an endodontist at the time and living on her own, had just broken up with her longtime boyfriend. Dori's twin sister, more mature socially, introduced her to the joint.

"It was a popular spot for our age group," Dori, known among her peers as "Miss Personality," recalled. "They had a DJ, and that was a big deal. We all just wanted to dance and be social. It was a great time going on back then," Dori said.

Ken walked through the front door of the Rail Road Inn into Dori's life sometime in October 1983. Ken wanted to be discreet, but he had "that cop look." And it had an effect on Dori's friends and coworkers who also partied at the Rail Road Inn.

"They all wanted to know what he did. Ken would say, 'I work construction.' He was a tight-lipped guy, and he just wanted to be a regular person."

The Pointer Sisters song "I'm So Excited" was playing the night Ken and Dori first kissed.

It was on December 25 of '83 that Ken made the next move.

"He called me to ask how my Christmas was. I'm Jewish. I didn't know what to say, so I said, 'Hold on a minute.' Then, I asked my twin how she thought I should respond."

"Chill out," she said. "Just say, 'I'm Jewish.'"

Ken took the reply in stride: "I want to know if you want to go out to the movies."

Her twin said, "Go for it." And Dori did.

The next night the couple made it to the theater where they watched *Sudden Impact* starring Clint Eastwood as the vigilante cop Dirty Harry. "I wasn't very romantic," said Ken.

Ken spent most of the night rubbing Dori's arm. "He liked me a lot," she recalled.

On Valentine's Day of '84, Ken let Dori know how he felt. He gave her a charm bracelet with an NYPD badge on it.

"He said I was going to be the mother of his children."

The couple was inseparable.

"We hung out with the people in the 88th. There was so much true love and affection between us, and Ken was the sweetest guy. He'd open my door. He was such a gentleman."

The new lifestyle suited Ken, he felt right at home. Sadly, It wasn't going to last. The transfer Ken put in on day one at the 88th was approved. He was headed back to the Seven Five. One year after arriving in idyllic Clinton Hill, Ken was packing his bags for a return to the Land of Fuck.

Upon arrival back in the old unit, Ken was cheered by fellow officers, who wondered why the hell anyone would want an assignment in East New York. Ken felt the Seven Five was his home. He belonged there and was happy to return.

With five years on the job, I was now one of the most senior men in the precinct. I went into roll call and checked out what officers were in which squads. Squad One was the most senior men and the officers I started with five years earlier. Squad

Two was about a year or two behind, obviously less experienced. Squad Three was all young officers that already had a bad reputation. Squad Three had no senior officer to set the pace and show the younger officers the way. Although from my experience senior officers weren't always a good influence anyway. Squad Three did have a leader though—Dowd.

I had my choice of squads, and I chose scooter one where I hooked right up with my old partner Frank Essig. He didn't last long and got transferred to Coney Island for the summer detail. The officers transferred to Coney Island for summer detail were usually a discipline problem that the CO wanted to get rid of for a few months. The detail was a well-known "dumping ground" in the department used by police commanders to get discipline problems out of their commands and beyond their responsibility—at least for the summer.

To officers it was like a vacation from the nightmarish Seven Five. Hanging out on the famous boardwalk all summer long eating and drinking for free. Where do I sign up?

Ken and Dori got married on August 3, 1985, at the Crest Hollow Country Club out on the Jericho Turnpike in Long Island, just past the sales lot for Extreme Exotics, a Ferrari Dealer.

"It was a huge wedding," Dori said. "It was the *creme de la creme*. Ken was so happy."

Ken's buddies and their wives accepted Dori into their clique.

"His friends loved me, and I loved them back," she said.

Ken soon partnered up with Michael Healy. The duo drank together from the beginning to the end of most shifts and held several contracts together in the Seven Five Precinct. Their partnership would be highlighted by the Eleanor Bumpurs case, not because they were involved in the Bronx woman's shooting, but because the NYPD officers union staged a work slowdown related to the case.

The details of the Bumpurs shooting, which took place on October 29, 1984, resonate today.

A sixty-six-year-old resident of the Bronx, Bumpurs, a 300-pound, mentally ill woman, was five months behind in her eighty-eight dollars a month rent when a group of police officers with shields, bullet proof vests, and riot helmets broke down her door intent on carrying out her eviction.

Words were exchanged, and a struggle ensued. At one point Bumpurs grabbed a ten-inch kitchen knife and slashed at Officer John Elter. Stephen Sullivan, Elter's partner, shot Bumpurs twice with a 12-gage shotgun at close range. The first shot struck Bumpurs's hand. The second caught her in the chest. She dropped to the floor of her shabby apartment and bled out.

The Bumpurs case was one of several such incidents that elevated racial tensions in New York City in the 1980s. Others included the death of MTA driver Willie Turks in 1982 and the 1983 arrest and death of Michael Stewart while in police custody.

New Yorkers and their police department also had to deal with the story of "Subway Vigilante" Bernard Goetz, a Queens man who shot four men on the subway just before Christmas 1984.

In the midst of it all was the Bumpurs case. Her death

caused an uproar and led to a grand jury indictment of Sullivan on charges of second-degree murder.

A grand jury indicted Sullivan for reckless manslaughter. Two lower courts rejected the indictment, but the state Supreme Court reversed and ordered a trial on the question of the second shot.

That led officers to take action. Their union instituted a work slowdown. Ultimately Sullivan was acquitted.

One swing shift during the slowdown the precinct was already backlogged with fifty or sixty jobs when Ken and Healy started their tour.

There was no way to clear the workload nor did anyone want to. As it got dark we parked near a bodega and went inside for a few drinks with a rookie named George Jackman. The rookie was basically running around on a foot post answering radio runs, on his own. That was stupid dangerous on his part, and Healy and I felt it our duty to teach this kid the right way to do police work. With the slowdown underway, the time was right.

After a few drinks we closed the store and turned out the lights so as not to be disturbed. Then we continued to drink by candlelight with the owner. After spending our entire meal hour drinking I called central dispatch over the telephone and let them know that we were out of service for "mechanical reasons." The reason for doing this was so central was aware of our status and wouldn't call for us over the air. So Healy, I, the rookie, and the store owner continued to drink by candle light.

Eventually the candle went out. The rookie attempted to relight the candle by sticking his hand inside the glass jar but the match upside down burnt his hand instead. Healy, being drunk and obnoxious, yells "You can't do anything! Give me that." It was very Oliver Hardy sounding.

Healy, without thinking because he's drunk, turns the jar upside down and begins to explain how the match won't burn his hand. Instead the hot wax pours out on Healy's shirt, tie, and hand.

Healy was yelling and screaming while the rookie and I were hysterically laughing. If you look today there are probably still wax marks on his tie. From that day on Mike Healy was known as "Waxman."

The nicknames, some crude, others nonsensical, were part of the milieu. Most of the officers had them. Some made sense, some didn't. There was Lardass, Squatbody, Duke, Brownman, Wethead, Marbles, Doctor, the Colonel, and Johnny Aces working various shifts.

Healy was the longest partnership I had. After about two years he left on a transfer to the 123rd Precinct in Staten Island where he lived. As senior man having an available seat in my sector, I was able to choose who would fill Healy's vacancy.

Since I trusted George Jackman, he

became my next partner. It didn't last long. Just before our partnership, Jackman had been involved in an on-duty shooting and was arrested for assault in the first degree. As far as I was concerned someone in the district attorney's office was trying to make a name for themselves at election time. They must have thought it was good politics to prosecute a police officer. But this perp had a gun when he was shot. I don't see how it was anything other than a justified shooting.

Which was much like what happened with the Officer Sullivan case, except Jackman's perp survived.

Jackman's perp was given a pass and turned state's witness. When he was a state's witness, the perp got arrested twice in the Seven Five. Both times he got cut loose because he was a state's witness. That's justice for you.

It was a good shoot. But with Jackman out. My car was open. Michael Dowd and I became partners. When Jackman returned to the Seven Five he was bitter and burned out.

# CHAPTER 12. PROFESSIONAL COURTESY

In the history of the New York Police Department, 1986 was not a good year. Murders, rapes, and robberies soared. In the Seven Five, officials documented a 12 percent spike in violent crimes. In the neighboring Seven Seven, the rate rose by 9.5 percent.

New York City Police Inspector Raymond Kelly, who headed the police department's Office of Management Analysis and Planning, told reporters gathered outside his office that March that he was baffled. Places like Washington Heights, where dealers sold crack out in the open was the worst—there were seventy-two murders in the 34th Precinct alone in 1986.

"It's hard to get trends out of this, other than we think there's a definite trend with drug-related homicide," Kelly said at the time.

In reality, the shitstorm was like a Southern California wildfire fueled by Santa Ana winds. Only this storm got its energy from cocaine—plain and simple. According to statistics, just 7 percent of homicide victims in 1981 had cocaine in their bloodstream at the time they died. By the mid-1980s, nearly 70 percent of homicide victims were high on coke when they were murdered. This clearly showed one thing: Plenty of people were enjoying coke, and a lot of those people were being murdered.

It was easier for Kelly to pretend there was no discernible trend, except he knew it wasn't just the skels who were dealing cocaine.

In May of 1986, Officer Henry Winter, one of Ken's former colleagues in the 77th Precinct, was arrested by

Internal Affairs investigators on suspicion of bribery and officer misconduct. It was a fancy way of saying he and his partner, Tony Magno, were dope-peddling thieves.

The case—as many often are—was made with the help of an informant. It grew when cops began to rat on brother officers.

The dominoes that were stacked against Winter and Magno began to fall with the arrest of Benny Burwell. A guy who paid his bills on time, Burwell was a coke dealer in the 77th Precinct who believed his goodwill toward the officers patrolling his sector—designated Ida John or IJ—would equal a "Get Out of Jail Free Card" if he was ever caught dealing or holding.

Sure Winter and Magno took Burwell's dough, but they did nothing to protect him from other cops. It proved to be a costly mistake.

A good cop caught Benny with a pound of coke. Benny first tried to bargain. It didn't work. Then he tried to bribe. That didn't work either. Benny wasn't about to dig a bigger hole for himself once he realized he was getting nowhere with the pigheaded sonofabitch who arrested him.

Because he didn't want to face the music—or a significant state prison sentence—Benny played "Let's Make a Deal" with the Brooklyn district attorney. When Benny told DA Elizabeth Holtzman he's was working with Winter and Magno, she not only believed him, but got Special Prosecutor Charles J. Hynes involved. Hynes's office had been established in the wake of Serpico and Knapp. The Seven Seven scandal marked its first big case.

Winter was nabbed by IA cops after he spent the day fishing at his favorite watering hole. They convinced Winter to get Magno to turn himself in and become a rat.

Together the two NYPD cops recorded several conversations with fellow officers in the precinct they called

"The Alamo." As the dirty cops committed the details of their crimes to audio tape, the chain of dominoes began to fall hard. Ultimately thirteen police officers were indicted in what would become known as the "Buddy Boys" scandal. The last domino to fall was Winter's friend, Officer Brian O'Regan, an oddball who lived at home with his mother and never quite fit in with the other cops in the precinct.

Rather than turn himself in for arraignment, forty-one-year-old O'Regan, dressed in jeans, a sweater, and a blue T-shirt emblazoned with the words "The Alamo," checked into a seedy sex motel on Route 109 in Lindenhurst, composed a suicide note, and ate his gun—a .25 auto.

The motel was everything you might imagine. Low slung and perfumed with the dank smell of stale cigarettes and cheap coffee, it was surrounded by a liquor store, a small used car lot, and a tarot card reader known as Psychic Barbara. Nobody could have foreseen O'Reagan's handwritten confession.

"Good morning. I missed my appointment," his fifty-page suicide note began. "I cannot swim in a cesspool. Can you? I will not turn. No. Never. I won't turn on another cop. The precinct is hell."

Just before his death, O'Regan explained to *New York Post* reporter Mike McAlary that he couldn't resist the temptation of bribery and theft. He confessed to McAlary that he felt guilty and depressed by the whole scenario and admitted taking bribes, selling drugs, and doing things that ashamed him.

As a law enforcement officer, O'Regan earned seven citations for his police work and a commendation for bravery because he single-handedly stopped a stolen car and arrested two armed men at gunpoint. As a dead man O'Regan earned everlasting renown as the New York cop who blew his brains out in a cheap room at the Pines Motor Lodge in

Lindenhurst rather than wind up in prison with perps, pervs, and psychopaths.

O'Reagan's act got some attention. Hynes, the special prosecutor, knew instinctively that the Seven Seven didn't stand alone when it came to being corrupt. He went so far as to warn NYPD Commissioner Benjamin Ward that the illegality of cocaine was leading to widespread malfeasance on the streets. And Hynes suspected that the Seven Five might be more screwed up than the Seven Seven. Ward, more concerned about politics and optics, refused to approve additional corruption investigations. With O'Reagan dead and the Buddy Boys about to be prosecuted, Ward felt he had little to lose.

Hynes had good reason to suspect something was amiss in the Seven Five. Brooklyn North's Internal Affairs Division had several cops under surveillance and were logging record numbers of corruption complaints from citizens. Unfortunately, Ward's refusal to take action often left IAD investigators with nothing but a pad, a pair of binoculars, and a shredder as their only tools.

Investigators like IAD's Joseph Trimboli complained about their work conditions, but for the most part they were mocked as Inspector Clouseaus and ridiculed for their inept attempts to catch suspected bad cops. Nonetheless, Hynes set his sights on Michael Dowd.

Dowd first caught the attention of IAD in 1985. Their growing notebook had some interesting entries. In one case he was accused of harassing and threatening his wife. In another incident he was accused of hooking up with prostitutes at a bar in East New York.

The allegations wouldn't have been hard to prove. Several of the cops who participated in Dowd-led orgies with crack-smoking hookers took photos of the festivities and passed them around the station house. Even with solid evidence available to detectives, both of the early corruption investigations into Dowd were closed and labeled unfounded by NYPD brass.

In March of 1986, Deputy Inspector Kevin Farrell reported Dowd and his then-partner Gerard Dubois to IAD on suspicion of stealing "money from drug dealers, prisoners, and deceased persons."

There were many examples of Dowd and his crew taking scores. Some of them were massive. Most of the details have been shared many times by officers familiar with the events. Ken learned about the exploits from Dowd himself.

While doing routine patrol Dowd and another cop get waved down by a Jamaican woman who stated her lazy ass husband just locked her out of the house. She wanted to go back, pack a bag, and go to her mother's home a few blocks away. Dowd and the other officer go to the front door. They can hear the husband saying "I told you woman, I have business."

For some reason, the husband opens the door. He gets a look at the police officers in their blue uniforms and yells, "Nooooo!"

Dowd and his partner muscle their way in, and sitting there on the living room coffee table are pounds and pounds of weed and cash. The dealer had just received a delivery and was restocking.

As he was taking it all in, Dowd makes the Jamaican dealer an offer too good to refuse: He won't arrest the dealer and will leave him some of the pot. Everything else now belongs to the

NYPD (wink, wink). Before leaving with
the loot and the dope, Dowd tells the
Jamaican man he will go to jail for sure
if his old lady has any more trouble.

Trimboli caught the case, but was unable to substantiate
any of the allegations. The higher-ups still sensitive about
what happened in the Seven Seven decided that Dowd and
his partner would be paired with other police department
miscreants, misfits, and oddballs on a Coney Island detail.

Even though he was at the amusement park for the
summer, back in the Seven Five, Dowd's crew of criminal-
minded cops was already formed. Besides his partner
Gerard Dubois, Dowd, by his own admission, said he could
could count on officers Henry "Chickie" Guevara, Jeffrey
Guzzo, Brian Spencer, Walter Yurkiw, Henry Jackson, and
others. Members of his crew routinely stole money and
drugs from street dealers and radio run locations. Dowd's
crew was scoring at every opportunity they could get and
passing some of the proceeds on to Mikey D. It worked like
a classic mob money scheme, with Dowd as godfather and
the other officers in his squad filling various roles as capos,
lieutenants, and consiglieres.

By the fall of '84, his Coney Island tour over, Dowd
was eager to start scoring again. His return in September
coincided with the departure of Ken's partner, George
Jackman. Since neither Ken nor Dowd had a partner, roll
call began placing them in the same sector. Ken hated it, but
there were few options.

It wasn't just the brass that mistrusted Dowd. Among
cops that weren't members of his crew, Dowd had a bad
reputation, and Ken had no real desire to work with him.
When they were in the car together, Dowd would constantly
brag about his scores. He knew Ken wouldn't talk. No one

would. Snitches get stiches.

Janice Hemmington,[3] an officer who was assigned to Brooklyn in the '80s and '90s, said a code of silence was powerfully enforced among the NYPD's rank and file.

"Who wants a rat jacket? The NYPD brass was completely unable to investigate corruption. There was no such thing as a confidential informant. You think I'd report Dowd or any of those guys? No way. Not smart."

Corrupt cops routinely told investigators they were unafraid of being turned in by other officers.

"It was the Blue Wall of Silence," former NYPD officer Bernard "The Mechanic" Cawley said. "Cops don't tell on cops. And if they did tell on them, just say if a cop decided to tell on me, his career's ruined. He's going to be labeled as a rat. So if he's got fifteen more years to go on the job, he's going to be miserable because it follows you wherever you go. And he could be in a precinct. He's going to have nobody to work with. And chances are if it comes down to it, they're going to let him get hurt."[4]

Former Officer Kevin Hembury agreed.

"If you're labeled a rat, especially early in your career, you're going to have a difficult time for the remainder of your career in the New York City Police Department. You do not want to be labeled a rat. You will be the recipient of bad practical jokes, even things more serious than practical jokes. Then, to leave or request to leave the environment that you were in, wouldn't be the end of this labeling that you had. Phone calls would be made to wherever your final destination was in the department. Your name traveled with

---

3   Not her real name

4   Anatomy of Failure: A Path for Success (The Mollen Commission Report) The City of New York Commission to Investigate Allegations of Police Corruption and the Anti-Corruption Procedures of the Police Department

you. It was something you couldn't shake."[5]

It wasn't that Ken hadn't seen corruption or even participated in out-of-policy favors, but none of it was on the scale of what Dowd was doing. Ken knew the code of silence and abided by it.

At that time, the 75th Precinct was an open air supermarket for drugs, especially Pitkin Avenue. Every day, drugs were sold pretty much right out in the open. Friday and Saturday nights the kids from the suburbs would come into Brooklyn. They would buy their drugs and return home. At that time, dust, heroin, and coke were top of the list. You could get any of them somewhere on Pitkin.

It was up to the Street Narcotics Enforcement Unit, known as SNEU, to catch the corner boys and their customers.

That unit was about making overtime for the cops and posting numbers and stats for the bosses. Everyone knows drugs sales aren't going to stop as long as there are drugs available. Arresting buyers and sellers only results in a new seller and new buyers.

Occasionally someone from my hometown would get snatched up and use my name. By the time I arrived the user would be sitting handcuffed in the back of a patrol car.

"He said he's your friend," the arresting officer would usually say, while

5   Ibid

shining a flashlight into the back of the patrol car.

"It's cool. You can let him go."

More often than not my acquaintance would be sent home. Now I owe this officer. And he knows he can trust me if he needs a favor. Professional courtesy is what cops call it.

The courtesy worked anywhere in New York.

My youngest brother Chris had a bad drug habit growing up. Being the youngest of three boys he grew up in a fast crowd of older kids. At fourteen or fifteen he had a habit of sneaking out and taking whichever car he could get.

One evening he had my grandmother's car. It was a green four-door Ford Fairmont. My brother had a car load of delinquents with him and they were cruising around town getting high. When he got to a school yard hangout he lost control of the car crashing into the two-story chain-link schoolyard fence. He ripped down about thirty feet of fence, and the car ended up standing straight up on its rear bumper resting against what fence remained.

Some of his buddies ran to my parents' house to get my other brother John, who was eighteen at the time. They wanted him to take the blame for the accident since he had a license. John managed to get Chris out and away from the scene. He attempted to get into the car and

get it down when cops from the 105th
Precinct arrived.

The cops put my brother in the rear of
the patrol car and began the paperwork.

"John Eurell? Do you know Ken Eurell?"

"Yeah, that's my brother."

"Your brother? No worries, we'll just
write it up as a simple accident. I use
to work with Ken in the Seven Five. How
is he?"

Someone cracked open a cold one.

"Here relax, have a beer with us."

Ken had seen more than professional courtesies extended
to brother officers. He knew about guys who pocketed
money from dead bodies or stole from drug dealers. But it
was mostly petty stuff.

One partner I had during my first pass
through the Seven Five was later fired when
the person he stole some drugs and money
from reported him and his partner. They
denied ever stopping the car, but there
was undeniable proof they did because
one of them left his police department-
issued hat in the complainant's car.

After the Buddy Boys story broke, Squad Three in the
Seven Five, which was led by Dowd, was disbanded. Clearly
the brass wasn't taking chances on a second drug scandal
being made public.

A few of Dowd's buddies like Guevara and Dubois quit
the department fearing they would be arrested as well. Dowd
hung around. It was then that officers began to think he might
be a rat. Dowd said he was betting on the department not

wanting another scandal anytime soon.

I asked some friends what they thought about me partnering with him.

Every one of them said the same thing: "Don't do it. He'll just get you in trouble."

It wasn't just one person warning me. It was a fucking policeman's glee club of voices all telling me that being partnered with Dowd was more than just a stupid idea, it was a really fucking stupid idea.

# CHAPTER 13. MIKE THE COP

In the late 1980s, crooked cops in the New York Police Department had become a different breed than their counterparts of bygone eras. Corruption had grown. Cops weren't just taking money to look the other way when a petty street crime was being committed. They were in direct competition with the street thugs and organized criminals that ruled New York's underworld.

Suddenly Joe Citizen was a victim of the very police force he believed was protecting him.

Psychologists who studied the NYPD in the 1980s found that overtime, as well as the constant and repeated exposure to temptation in the high crime and drug-crazed precincts, wore down the values and principles of many good cops. Over time even the best cops became more susceptible to corruption. It was especially true when the culture accepted and protected the predators and bad cops.

Early on in his partnership with Mike, Ken got a sense of how far Dowd had gone away from accepted values toward absolute corruption. The first glimpse came during a weekly poker game at Ken's house. The group played Texas Hold 'em with one- to two-dollar stakes. High rollers might call the game dull.

"At the end of a very bad night you might lose a hundred dollars," Ken noted.

Dowd was invited but arrived about an hour late.

```
    He sits down at the table and pulls
out a stack of bills that could choke a
horse. It was like everything suddenly
```

stopped for a moment while we all stared at the money. It was one of those things that you never forget. None of us had that kind of money to blow.

The wad was part of Dowd's larger plan to test Ken. It was something he did each time he was assigned a new partner. He wanted to see how far a partner would go. Usually it started with minor incidents like taking free food or drinking on duty. Once Dowd knew that his partner would engage in minor misconduct, he would take it to the next level, offering to share in the proceeds of whatever scam he had going on at the time.[6]

Once Dowd and I were steady partners he went to work testing me to see how much it would take before I would cross the thin blue line that separates cops and criminals. Almost immediately Dowd started to talk about making money. How much money was out there and how we can get our hands on it.

All Mike did was talk about money 99 percent of the time. The other 1 percent was about pussy. Like money, Mike Dowd wanted it.

Within a year of the 77th's Buddy Boys scandal, Dowd's flamboyance continued to grow. He drove a flashy red Corvette into the precinct every day. He wore expensive clothes, threw outrageous parties, and routinely hired

---

6   Anatomy of Failure: A Path for Success (The Mollen Commission Report)The City of New York Commission to Investigate Allegations of Police Corruption and the Anti-Corruption Procedures of the Police Department

limousines to ferry his crew from East New York to Atlantic City. He especially enjoyed gambling at the newly opened Trump Plaza, a 600-room hotel that opened next to Caesars Atlantic City in 1984 and had eighty-five high roller suites that catered to guys with flash rolls like Dowd.

Dowd refused to conceal his lifestyle, and rather than repulse fellow cops, it had the effect of turning them on. More than one hump in the Seven Five begged Dowd for an invitation to join his crew.

At first with Ken around, Dowd talked about drinking on the job. When Ken didn't react, Dowd whipped out photos of on-duty cops partying at The Pool with a couple of prostitutes.

While the officers drank, the two hookers danced naked on top of their patrol cars doing unmentionable things with a nightstick. I didn't have much more of a reaction than a raised eyebrow. Then, Dowd let me in on more brazen acts and explained to me that if I would have hooked up with him sooner I could have made some serious money.

I wasn't exactly sure what Dowd was talking about. In fact, I had no real clue at all. The only extra money I had earned outside the police department was working for a security firm while off-duty.

Another officer from the Seven Five was neighbors with the owner of a private security firm. It was great that he was able to get off-duty security jobs for his friends who worked in the 75th Precinct.

Some of the jobs were working for the Metropolitan Opera in the city, the MET, as it is known in NY. First I worked gigs like the Russian ballet. It got interesting when I was asked to work during the filming of a two-night special Robin Williams was filming for HBO. We were able to go backstage and see the celebrities that turned out to tell Williams he did a good show.

The second night on that job, Madonna came through, followed by Sean Penn. He was guiding her with his hands on her shoulders. Behind them was Robert DeNiro. All of them were practically rubbing against us as they walked past and headed to the green room backstage.

When they had gone we debated whether or not Madonna was attractive.

The guy who got us the gig thought Madonna was butt ugly. One of the guys on the detail thought he was crazy. He was in love with her. I thought she was OK. Any attractiveness that she had was enhanced by her celebrity. "Butt ugly" wasn't my opinion.

Sean Penn seemed super protective of Madonna. I couldn't tell if any of them was fucked up on drugs or cocaine. They walked by very quickly.

Robin Williams, on the other hand, was coked up. And, of the celebrities, he was the only one who spoke with us. He was wired and literally banging off the hallway walls from side to side pretending he was a cop holding his hands and fingers like it was a gun. I wanted to jump in the limo with him and continue the night but I acted professional. I wanted to keep the job. Fifty dollars an hour back in 1986 to do celebrity security was phenomenal.

Dowd told Kenny he didn't have to be a scrub security guard making peanuts on the side. In fact, he said, there were all sorts of scams and scores taking place. In one instance, Dowd told how a call about a burglary turned into a score that netted him and a couple of his buddies— including Chickie Guevara, who had already left the force—the equivalent of a year's salary.

"This was the big one," Guevara later recalled.

As Guevara tells it, Dowd, who was on patrol with another officer, responded to a call for service. Two women were attempting to break into an apartment and get their clothes. They explained they had to break in because the boyfriend of one of the women was arrested. The apartment keys were with him in the lock-up. Anti-Crime Unit, plainclothes detectives who do gang operations, also arrived on the scene.

The plainclothes officers arrested the two women for burglary. Dowd entered the apartment and found two large plastic garbage bags filled with cash.

Witnesses said Dowd managed to con the plainclothes cops into leaving the money—and they did. Dowd sealed the apartment and rushed to a payphone to call Guevara. Thirty minutes later Guevara was on the scene dressed like a detective and holding a fake badge. He and another former officer entered the apartment and removed the cash—just like that. Later there was an argument over how it should be split.

People who have never had money would think, "If I can only get a few thousand dollars everything will be alright. I can pay off all my bills and put some away for a rainy day." These guys have clearly passed that stage, but more money is still wanted. Greed takes over at this point. It's like sharks in a feeding frenzy.

They all knew it was proceeds from drug sales. I'm sure they didn't think of it as stealing either. The arrested drug dealer wasn't going to get it, and if they turned it in, the money would just go to the city.

A few days later the plainclothes detectives asked Dowd if he ever went back and took the money. He said no. That was the end of the follow up.

Guevara said the adrenaline rush that came with the heist fueled his addiction for more action.

Now it was Ken's turn.

The incident that first turned me occurred so fast I wasn't even aware of it. The deal went down when we were called to the scene of a burglary.

As we arrive on the scene, Dowd and I are met by a teenage girl who is afraid to enter her house because the front door has been broken in. Her parents aren't home, and she just returned from school.

Dowd and I enter, search, and clear the house, and discover that the criminal is gone.

"Do you know if your parents have any money or jewelry that might be missing?" Dowd asked.

"If there is anything, it's on the top shelf of my parents' bedroom closet," she answered.

Dowd, I, and the girl go to the bedroom. Dowd takes down some boxes and does some reaching around.

"Nothing there. They must have got it," Dowd said to the victim as he pocketed $800 he found under a Bible on the shelf.

Another unit arrived on scene and began to take a police report. We took off. About a mile down the road Dowd pulls a hundred-dollar bill out of his pocket.

"What's that?" I said.

"You didn't even see me take it did you?" Dowd said. "I got 200. This one's for you."

For Ken, the theft and its aftermath was a moment of truth. He weighed his options.

I could have said no to Mike and kept my mouth shut but would have been considered just as guilty. I could have turned Mike over to Internal Affairs, which would be committing department suicide. My only choice was to take the money. The one hundred dollars sat in the top of my locker for weeks. I felt like if I didn't spend it I could always go back.

At the time I would have never thought of it. I'm sure now that this has to be common among police departments. This is something that exists where no one—including the rightful owner—would suspect the police. A home is broken into; the police show up and take what the criminal missed. The owner just assumes the criminal who broke in took the valuables.

If Ken felt bad about how it all went down, his partner was giddy. A few weeks later, when Mike met a car stereo dealer named Baron Perez, Ken and Mike's partnership was on a whole new footing.

# CHAPTER 14. CRACK WHORES
# AND CONTRACT KILLERS

It was close to 1:00 a.m. the first time Mike Dowd walked into Baron Perez's car stereo shop on a warm night in June 1987. Perez, who had a reputation as New York's best car stereo guy was hard at work, which wasn't unusual. But, Dowd didn't know that. He would soon learn that the shop on Atlantic Avenue at the northern edge of the 75th Precinct was constantly busy. There wasn't a person in the neighborhood who didn't know Baron or his immaculate, graffiti-free stereo shop.

Even though it was too late for the shop to be open, it wasn't the lights that attracted Dowd's attention. Instead, he had seen a beautiful woman walk into Baron's store at a time when everything else in the neighborhood—even the McDonald's next door—was closed. Dowd, pussy hound that he was, was drawn to her like a mosquito to warm blood coursing through the veins of a thin-skinned fat man. He admitted as much to Perez once he entered the shop.

It was understood that any woman out at that hour was looking to score. Crack had that effect on people. Perez recalled those years as horrific. He'd seen mothers sell their seven-year-old daughters' virginity to dope dealers in exchange for a five-minute high.

"That shit was so powerful that women would suck dick for two dollars and think nothing about it," he said.

Perez's corner of the world was a window into the depravity wrought by desperation and a compulsion to feel good, if only for five minutes.

Perez, a dread-locked, lights-skinned Dominican who

immigrated to the US in 1967, had pretty much seen it all by 1987.

"You could get someone killed for ten or fifteen dollars," Perez recalled. "That was all it took sometimes, especially if the guy you hired really wanted to get a rock."

Perez, who is tall but skinny, recalled a neighborhood guy he nicknamed Bubba. Bubba was six-foot-five, 300 pounds, and always getting picked on by guys in the neighborhood who had the man running all sorts of errands. Perez said he felt sorry for Bubba and always made sure he had enough to eat and decent clothes.

One day some detectives came to Perez's shop with a photo of Bubba.

"Mr. Perez, we're looking for somebody. Do you know this guy?"

"Why do you want him?"

"We just want to talk to him."

"No, seriously. Why do you want to talk to him?"

"That's between us and him, sir. Do you know him?"

Perez declined to answer. He later found out what the police wanted.

"This guy Bubba, he killed people for drug dealers. He would shoot somebody for one or two hundred dollars. He was a paid killer in the ghetto. You'd never know it the way those other guys picked on him."

So when Dowd, a cop, came into the shop looking for a strawberry—street slang for a prostitute hooked to crack cocaine—Perez wasn't too surprised. There'd be no action though. The woman happened to be Perez's wife.

"Basically he tried to pick up my wife," Perez recalled. "It was an ignorant move, but I wasn't too shocked. My wife was a beautiful girl."

After he got over the shock about what he had foolishly attempted, Dowd struck up a conversation and soon understood why the shop was open late—Perez had work to do. Big time players needed sound systems in their rides. Perez was the guy they trusted to do it right and keep his mouth shut about it.

Dowd saw something he liked—the possibility of making money.

"He said I looked like one of the presidents," Perez recalled. "Lincoln, Washington, Grant. You know, the presidents on the money."

Given the intricacies of New York's drug dealing network, the comment made sense.

Dominicans dominated the mid-levels of New York's coke trade. Across the East River, the Wild Cowboys kept their Manhattan and Bronx rivals in check with the help of Francisco Medina, a psychopathic contract hitman known as "Freddie Krueger."

In Brooklyn, La Compania was connected to Colombian wholesalers. The Dominicans sold large quantities of coke to a wide variety of customers, including street gang entrepreneurs and the top nightclubs' in-house drug dealers. The bosses were not intimidated by rules, laws, or law enforcement. Officials allege that Maximo Reyes, a Compania lieutenant, once set up a cop for execution by luring him to a payphone with a fake 911 call.

"Talk to people who were in East New York in those times. They'll tell you that it was hardcore," Perez said. "When you see someone who made it through those days, that's someone you don't want to mess with. That is a person that has seen it all and done it all."

The streets were mean, tough, and violent, but there was something very different about the men at the top, according to Perez.

"A friend I have, I was close to this guy, he wants to be the only guy in town. He had forty blocks, corners where he was dealing heroin and coke. He was making $100,000 a day minimum. He looked like somebody's girlfriend that's how soft he was. He looked like a gay man. But, if he gave an order, that was it. No one ever argued with that guy. He had power. The street level dealers were mere posers by comparison," Perez said.

"I'd see these guys around; I'd call them GITs. You know what that means? 'Gangsters in Training.' Their look was tough, but they were bullshit compared to the real thing."

Baron could call on Reyes or Adam Diaz or La Compania head Jose "Chelo" Montalvo at any time because they were appreciative customers who admired his work.

"They all respected me. I had rules. No guns. No arguments. No talking about drugs in my shop. That's the way it had to be," Perez said.

A kid caught putting graffiti on Perez's building or those of his neighbors was quickly identified, apprehended, and compelled to make things right.

"Most times it would take less than eight hours to find who did it," Perez said. "And when he was caught, he'd have to paint the whole building."

Not only was Perez's shop off limits to violence and bluster. His block of Atlantic Avenue was off-limits too.

"A young kid shot somebody outside the bodega across the street. He shot the guy in the ass with a 9 mm.

"Why did he do it?

"He said the guy took his 8-ball jacket.

"After the shooting, the young kid came by my shop. 'I shot that guy in the ass, and I'm sorry Mr. Perez.' That was that."

Perez said the neighborhood respected him not only because he kept out of their business but was always kind and understanding.

"I was trained by a very powerful Jewish guy," Perez

said. "He made me realize that even though I was a minority I could be powerful. I never met a stranger. I understand you when I meet you. I know where you are coming from. And I never gave anything up."

Everyone in the neighborhood knew they could turn to Perez if they needed a favor.

"I helped everybody that came in. If they had trouble paying for a new stereo or an alarm, I let them pay me weekly."

Perez also said he was fortunate that he wasn't chained to the daily grind of East New York.

"I had a family and a life," he said. "I would go to the city, see a show, have a nice meal. I had other interests. At the same time I understood you have to be hard, but you have to help people in your community or else you are a prisoner. You gotta live like your neighbors in order to survive.

"I never did anything wrong or illegal. I worked hard for my family. What worked was that I could deal with the killers and I could deal with the police."

While Dowd suspected Baron Perez might hold the key to future earnings for him and Kenny, Perez said Dowd wanted to be sure he could trust him. So Dowd asked about having a beer cooler installed in his police cruiser. Baron figured out a way to do it and made sure it would avoid detection. In a matter of days the two men were discussing ways they could make money together.

Ken thought Baron was on the arm—police slang for a business owner who doled out favors to the neighborhood cops. He started bringing family cars around to have them outfitted with new stereos and alarm systems.

Dowd, I, and Perez became very friendly. Perez as a show of friendship to his new officer friends would install stereo and alarm systems in all our cars on the arm.

As Baron remembered it, Dowd eventually suggested setting up a meeting with La Compania. The cop explained he had information and other assistance that would be valuable to high-level drug dealers. A meeting followed.

Jose "Chelo" Montalvo came, looking to all the world as a slick metropolitan businessman who had a crew of stone cold killers dropping bodies like blown roses all over East New York.

Dowd told me he has a deal working with Perez that could bring us some serious money. Perez, fully trusted by all parties, would be the middleman between the local drug dealers and us. For $8,000 a week, La Compania would get information on how to better run their business. In exchange, Dowd and I would arrest or pass information to the narcotics division on the other drug dealers in the neighborhood. This would allow Perez's connection to get a stronghold in the Seven Five. Perez put the meeting together.

Dowd and Eurell staked out a bodega where Chelo's people did the majority of their business. They watched as runners, bagmen, and packagers worked in the open. They took notes.

Shortly after forwarding Dowd and Eurell's critique to La Compania, Perez called the officers to say he had something for them.

Dowd and I arrived at Perez's shop one afternoon after a day tour. Waiting there for us was a bag with $7,300.
Dowd was pissed off and screaming.
"What the fuck, Baron? The deal was for 8 large.'
What the fuck?

On the drive home to Long Island Ken thought, "Why turn away $3,650 that just falls into my lap for doing absolutely nothing?"
Dori was on the front steps of the couple's home in Babylon when Ken arrived. Some of her friends were there too. They sipped chilled wine and chatted in the warm weather waiting for their husbands to return home from the city.

There was a huge bulge of cash in my pocket when I got out of Dowd's car. I ushered the other wives away and brought Dori inside and showed her the wad.
I told my wife, "Don't ask; don't tell: Don't ask where the money came from; don't tell anyone we have it."
Dori was scared and frightened for us and what I was getting involved in.
Dowd was pissed. He didn't want to continue working for La Compania if they didn't pay us the full amount. Dowd told Baron that Chelo's people better pay.

They didn't take well to Dowd threatening them, and Perez was told that a contract was going to be put on Dowd's life. When Mike Dowd found out, it took him less than twenty-four hours to find Chelo and pull him over for a routine traffic stop.

> Chelo didn't know Dowd on sight. He just thinks it's some cop stopping him for a broken taillight or some such shit. Well Mike reads him the fucking riot act from hell, and it had the effect of scaring the shit out of Chelo. The contract was called off. We got our $700.

For his part, Baron Perez didn't like the sort of trouble a guy like Dowd brought down on everyone around him but agreed to get in touch with another dealer who would be happy to pay for police protection.

The man's name was Adam Diaz.

# CHAPTER 15. THE COLUMBIAN CONNECTION

Perez's shop was small. It had three small work bays that were always in action. Concerned that his cop friends had been burned, Perez arranged for them to meet Adam Diaz, who ran a competing organization. Diaz, a Dominican like Perez, got his shit straight from Columbia. It was the best product on the market, and both Diaz and Dowd knew it.

"I got contacted by Baron," Diaz said. "'A couple of cops want to see you.'"

Surviving in the game was a difficult proposition. The Colombians didn't take shit from anybody. Those who crossed the line found themselves at the business end of a murder contract. The very fact that Adam Diaz was alive and working meant he was a businessman who could be trusted with large quantities of product and money.

"A lot of my friends are dead or doing life in jail. I guess I was lucky," Diaz said.

In that environment the idea that a couple of street cops would be meeting with a high-level drug kingpin was absurd. But here they all were. Ken, Dowd, and Adam Diaz.

"I wasn't used to dealing with cops," Adam admitted. "But I knew they were going to propose something; I just didn't know what. Then then they contacted me through Baron, and we set up a meeting."

Ken was surprised by Adam's look and demeanor. Adam, who barely weighed one hundred pounds, arrived at the meeting and made an immediate impression. He was well-dressed, well-spoken, easy to like, and eager to do business.

"We met Adam in the back of Baron's shop at Atlantic and Van Siclan. He was small, not physically threatening at all."

Adam said he was impressed by what he saw.

"I looked at Dowd, and I saw gangster. I didn't see cop. I looked at Kenny, and all I saw was a cop. Pure cop."

If he was impressed, he also admitted to being a bit paranoid. The men who worked for Baron would see a known drug dealer working with cops. They could be up to anything. He could be ratting out an associate; he could be turning state's evidence; he could be undercover himself. Whatever the situation, a guy like Adam meeting with two known police officers wasn't necessarily good for appearances—or business for that matter—if word got out.

"I told Baron, 'With your guys working here, we got to do this in your office and lock the door. I don't want nobody seeing me with these cops.'"

Once inside the office, Dowd explained what he and Kenny could do and what they were looking for in exchange. The deal was nearly the same that they offered to La Compania and Chelo, only this time there would be no bullshit.

Again the two police officers would provide a range of security services to Diaz's operation. Those services included checking drug sales points for weaknesses, watching out for undercover busts, protecting the stash, and harassing the competition.

Diaz knew the assistance of two police officers could greatly help increase his drug profits. He also wanted the clout of police officers on his payroll.

There was no negotiation. No haggling. No raised voices. Just numbers.

Dowd simply laid it on the line, $24,000 cash to start and $8,000 every week after that.

Kenny wondered why not $25,000 to start and $10,000 a week? Those are, after all, round numbers that appealed to his obsessive compulsive side. Dowd pulled the number out of thin air and probably bid too low. Adam jumped at the offer.

> As part of our agreement, all payments would be through the mutually trusted Perez. That way Dowd, I, and Diaz who was a known drug trafficker wouldn't have to be seen together ever again.

Before leaving, the men set up a series of coded messages they could transmit to each other via beeper. The codes would provide Adam the information he had just purchased.

> One set of numbers meant shut down immediately because narcotics officers were in the area working that day.
> Another set of numbers let Diaz know it was safe to reopen for business. A third code let Adam know that he could conduct business as usual at all of his locations.

Ken and Dowd agreed to pay a broker fee to Baron Perez for putting the deal together.

> Dowd and I agreed to give Baron $2,000 each from the $24,000, so he took $4,000 from the initial deal. We also decided to give him $500 each from the $8,000 a week we would receive from Adam.

Ken's career was about to make a huge shift. No longer a cop who occasionally drank on duty, Officer Eurell was on the payroll of a notorious Brooklyn drug dealer, and it wasn't too bad.

The day we were going to get paid, I dropped off my wife and son at her grandmother's home, which was still in the 75th Precinct. I was pretty familiar with her place. During the years I was on duty I would stop by with my various partners to check up on her. More often than not she would have a big bowl of chicken and rice cooking for me. We'd sit down and eat some nice homemade cooking. It was a nice break from some crazy tours in the Seven Five.

On the day Ken and Dowd were getting money from Adam Diaz, their shift went by as slowly as Christmas Eve for a five-year-old. But just like Christmas, there was a present waiting for the officers when they got off duty.

At the end of the day tour, Dowd and I went to Perez's radio shop. The money was sitting there waiting for us. We sat there counting it in the stockroom before we left to be sure we weren't shorted this time. We gave Perez $2,000 each, $4,000 total for his help. We walked away with $20,000 and didn't even lift a finger. It felt great; nothing could get the smiles off our faces. We hadn't even done anything other than offer our help at that point.

Next stop was Dori's grandmother on the north end of the precinct. Dowd and Ken sat in front. Dori got the backseat.

Dowd was driving a crappy blue Hyundai east on the Southern State Parkway. He bought it cash with money he picked up on some other deals here and there. Dowd, being Dowd, was driving at breakneck speed out of the city. He had that Hyundai doing about a hundred miles an hour at a couple of points on the tree-lined state highway that connects Valley Stream to Eastern Long Island.

I put the money, which was in a brown paper bag, on the floor in the back. I asked Dori to reach into the bag and take out a couple of beers for Dowd and me.

Dori dutifully reached into the bag. Except there was no beer. Just cash. Lots of it. She let out a little shriek.

"Oh my God, Kenny! What's all this money?"

Dori remembered the moment well.

"I had to take a moment to get a grip on what was happening."

Sensing Dori might be anxious about the money, Dowd jumped in.

"How do you feel about that Dori?"

Dori didn't have time to answer. Right then we get pulled over for speeding by a fucking state trooper. Dowd pulls to the left on the fucking median of the parkway and jumps out. He starts running towards the trooper with his badge out, and he's shouting, "What the fuck? I'm on the job here."

Dowd wasn't really on the job, and he was really going about one hundred miles per hour.

The state trooper gave a friendly wave and let Dowd know everything would be fine.

"Have a nice evening. Be careful, sir."

Professional courtesy paid off once again. It was the first time, but not the only time, we were pulled over with money or drugs or drugs and money in the car.

Throughout the traffic stop Dori sat in the backseat with the money.

"I wasn't scared of being pulled over," she said. "After all, they were police officers. I was annoyed as hell though. Michael talked his way out very quickly, and we were back on the road, only now he was driving in a much better manner."

Ken put his arm on the back of his seat and turned toward Dori on the drive home. He promised everything would be fine.

"Seeing all that money left me queasy," she said.

More money followed. Diaz paid $8,000 each week. On time. In cash. Ken and Mike gave Baron Perez $500 each for collecting and holding the money.

The extra money gave Perez an opportunity to buy out his partner and open a much larger shop at Atlantic and Crescent. There Auto Sound City took over a former bus depot and opened its doors to newer, wealthier clients.

The Diaz money we were taking home was a huge increase from the $700 bi-weekly paycheck we each got for being one of New York's finest in the 1980s. It got so crazy there were weeks that Dowd forgot to pick up his paycheck.

Ken was taking exotic vacations; he and Dori bought all new appliances and ate out often. The couple went from a little Cape home to a brand new, custom-built, huge Hi-Ranch home with a full basement, in-ground swimming pool, a two-story deck, and a full garage.

Dori was always telling me to please stop. She would say, "I'd live with you in a trailer we don't need all this."

Even Ken's dad wondered if his son had turned the corner from cop to crook.

My father definitely suspected I was doing something, so his way of telling me to stop without actually coming out and saying it was to tell me about his boss's son who had a brand new Corvette get confiscated by police because of drugs. It was sort of a warning to me.

As he and Dowd grew closer, Ken began spending more time away from home and his growing addiction to easy money made it hard to get out of the Seven Five. There was always some new game, some new angle, some new profitable corruption.

None of this went unnoticed by Dowd's superiors at the NYPD, and Internal Affairs already had several files open on Officer Mike Dowd by the time he and Kenny became partners. The list of complaints was shocking. But, as if harkening back to the gaslight days of old New York, nothing was done. If someone in charge knew a bit of history, they might have ripped a page from the Lexow Commission Report issued all the way back in 1894:

*"The members of the Police Department were bound together by the cohesion of public plunder. They were not of the people. They did not belong to the people. They regarded themselves as separate and apart from the people."*

# CHAPTER 16. THE WHITE RABBIT

Dowd's downright criminality didn't go unnoticed, but it certainly went unpunished. Dowd had an explanation of his own for the behavior, an explanation perfectly in sync with what any New York cop would tell you as far back as 1894.

"It's 'us versus them out there.' ... The public are not going to beat us, the cops, in the streets. We can have our way when we put on the badge."

The behavior was part of the job.

"The first thing I learned to do on this job was lie. Once you learn to lie to cops, it's only a matter of time before you learn to steal," he added.

The NYPD assigned Joe Trimboli with the Field Internal Affairs Unit to monitor Dowd, which was sort of like being told to keep track of a runaway train, but don't talk about it.

By any measurement one could make, the NYPD is a Byzantine organization. The levels of bureaucracy often cause the organization to grow at a glacial pace if at all. NYPD's massive size made for a large org chart too. In the 1980s, a printed version of the department's explanation of its hierarchy measured eighteen-by-twenty-two inches.

FIAU, which consisted of cops assigned to each field service area, was a branch of the detective bureau, but—in theory—followed a separate chain of command. The Seven Five and the Seven Seven were each in the Brooklyn North Division.

Beat cops throughout NYPD viewed Internal Affairs cops as rats. Trimboli lived up—or down—to the expectations of his peers by going after dirty cops. It worked well enough for him when he was going after dope-dealing cops like Winter and O'Regan in the Seven Seven, but not well enough when he started looking at Dowd.

"You gotta ask the obvious question," said former New Jersey cop Fred Wolfson. "What was the difference? Why didn't they go after Dowd? Simple. They didn't want another scandal. Rather than deal with it and be humiliated in public, they just looked at it and then looked away. It was a political move designed for the top brass to keep their jobs."

It was almost as if the police commissioner insisted "There is no other corruption. Leave my department alone, my department is clean. I don't want to hear about any more corruption."

Maybe someone should have changed the Internal Affairs mission statement to read "See no evil. Hear no evil. Speak no evil." It would have been accurate.

Sets of desktop monkeys acting out the age-old line might even have been mandatory desktop ornaments, especially in the NYPD's halls of power at One Police Plaza. Internal Affairs stopped looking at drug cases involving cops and instead focused on allegations that included uniform violations, domestic violence, and insubordination.

"When I went to the commissioner with corruption cases, I felt like he wanted to shoot me," Internal Affairs head Daniel Sullivan admitted.

"Shit rolls downhill," noted ex-cop Wolfson, "and it all piled up on Trimboli's lap. Unlike his bosses, Trimboli swore to investigate the department's assholes—starting with Dowd."

"I was the last one you wanted to have looking, because I wasn't going to stop," said Trimboli. "I was going to just keep on coming until I proved or disproved what happened, and that was my mindset in every investigation. I'm not going to let politics come into play here, especially not with something as serious as drugs and cops. They just don't go together. It was totally contrary to what I felt morally obligated to do. To look the other way and let a corrupt cop exist on the streets, I couldn't do that. I took an oath. I couldn't look away."

Trimboli began following Dowd in 1986, when Dowd was on his Coney Island detail. Dowd gave the impression of being cocky and in control, but Trimboli believed Dowd was entirely full of shit as opposed to being merely full of shit.

Dowd sensed he was on IAD's radar, and when he thought he was being tailed, he often drove erratically to avoid leading the shoofly toward any location where a deal might be going down. It didn't matter. Through confidential informants and anonymous phone calls, Trimboli eventually discovered Baron Perez's Auto Sound City, Chelo's operation with La Compania on Fulton Street, and Adam Diaz's storefront cocaine mini mart on New Lots Avenue.

Looking into Dowd eventually led Trimboli to others in Dowd's social circle including Gerard Dubois, Walter Yurkiw, Dowd's brother Robert, and Henry Guevara. He learned they hung out with a guy named Joe Adonis, who was a member of Chelo's crew. He pieced together enough thread to figure out Dowd's crew frequented a neighborhood watering hole known as Bailey's Bar. The rundown dive occupied a seedy corner of the PathMark mini-mall in Starrett City.

Ken was familiar with Starrett City, a low-rent high-rise project partly owned by Donald Trump. He'd been there more than once.

Early on in my career, my partner and I got a call in Starrett City about shots fired. The caller told our dispatcher that a bullet had come through their apartment wall and lodged just above their baby's crib; a few inches lower and it would have killed the kid.

Anyway the parents were shaken and upset when we got there. We followed the path, and it led us next door. We go next door, and two young teen boys, brothers, Irish twins, like nine months apart. They were home alone. They had been playing with their father's guns.

The kids admitted that one of them fired off a rifle, and the bullet went through the apartment wall.

So we confiscated all the guns and took the kids to Spofford, a juvenile detention center in the Bronx. When my partner and I left we looked at each other and I said, "One day one of these kids will kill somebody."

Two years or so later a call comes over for shots fired, one victim down. I recognized the address, it was Starrett City. I told my partner as we rolled, "I called it."

Sure as shit when we get there one of the brothers did kill someone—his own brother.

Bailey's was just across the street from the Starrett City project towers.

The owner was a housing cop who welcomed officers—especially those in uniform. They parked their patrol cars out back and drank for free. Come in off duty and you'd pay for your beer or mixed drink or whatever. The bar was safe. The crew knew it, and Dowd's guys routinely divided up their loot and snorted coke with abandon. More than once the crew and their badge bunnies hooked up for orgies on the pool table or—when the pool table was occupied—they hit any one of the hourly rate hot-sheet motels on the Belt Parkway heading toward JFK Airport.

Even though it caused stress at home, Ken said it was important to spend on- and off-duty hours in the Seven Five. It was all about making money. He came into Trimboli's universe via an anonymous caller who told a detective that "Michael Dowd and Kenny Eurell are being paid by drug dealers."

Being involved with Chelo and then Adam's organization wasn't the only way Ken and Dowd were scoring.

There was an elderly man who sold heroin at the corner of Essex and Pitkin. Dowd had been watching the man sell the shit for years. We attempted to watch the dealer during work in order to find out where he lived. Unfortunately, between radio calls and the old dealer moving around, we were unable to pin him down. We began to refer to the old man as the "White Rabbit."

Dowd eventually turned to Chickie Guevara for help. Guevara and another ex-cop, who was still a member of Dowd's crew, put their own tail on the old man.

It took them a few days of following the White Rabbit, but they did finally pin him down to a block in Queens. The next day we sat on the block until the White Rabbit came home and we got his address. Now we needed a plan to get his dope and his money.

The Queens neighborhood is very congested with houses right on top of one another. Of course the easiest thing to do would be impersonate local cops. I typed up a fake warrant with the White Rabbit's name and address on it.

While downtown processing an arrest I grabbed a blank affidavit and added the necessary information with a typewriter. Dowd picked up a scanner with codes for the Queens precinct. Guevara bought point-to-point radios, and his former partner provided a freshly stolen license plate.

Even with all the bogus paperwork, our plan was to go in when the White Rabbit was out. That way there would be no problem. The warrant was needed in case other occupants were in the house. The next day we all met in a shopping center on Atlantic Avenue a few blocks away from the location. We went over the plan one more time: I was the driver; Dowd was in the passenger seat. The other two guys sat in back. We used Chickie's powder blue four-door Oldsmobile, which could easily pass for an unmarked police car.

After the first pass by the house I noticed a scooter cop writing a summons. After passing the house twice more to see if the cop had left (he didn't) the scooter cop hit his siren and motioned for me to pull over as we passed him. I pulled immediately to the right, just as

I would have done if I were actually in a plainclothes unit.

"License and registration," the scooter cop meant business as he approached the Oldsmobile. After all, the car was fitted with stolen plates.

"We're with Central Warrants," I responded, flashing the tin hanging around my neck.

"Then I pointed at Dowd and said, "That's Sergeant O'Neil."

The cop was concerned.

"Any way I can help you guys?"

"No the boss is just waiting for you to finish up so we can serve a warrant."

The scooter cop quickly finished his job and took off. There was a sigh of relief in the backseat. I circled the block again and double-parked in front of the White Rabbit's house. Chickie and his former partner jumped out and knocked on the front door of the first floor apartment. White Rabbit wasn't home, but his nephew was.

This made Chickie and his former partner get somewhat panic stricken. As soon as they exited the building empty-handed they ran out to the street and jumped in the backseat.

"GO! GO!" Chickie yelled. "GO!"

Dowd freaked out. His nasal voice was piercing and full of anger.

"What the fuck do you mean you didn't get anything?"

"We couldn't do it; someone was home"

Chickie's buddy explained.

"Jesus Christ! That's why we got a fucking warrant!" Dowd yelled.

I drove back to the house and broke the door down with Guevara. The nephew was gone. So was the money, and so were the drugs. It was one of the few times we came up short.

It wasn't just drugs Ken and Mike went for, they also took guns, often helping out Adam Diaz's workers when they needed a piece for protection. In one case Dowd used the gift of a gun to exploit one of Diaz's guys.

He began getting ounces of coke from the guy.

At first this was a point of friction between me and Mike. Dowd was picking up the cocaine in full uniform and on-duty. I didn't want to be involved with the drugs in any way, which, looking back, doesn't really make any sense. This too would change with time. Dowd was selling most of the coke without giving me any of the money from the sales.

Dowd soon began using cocaine in the open and on the job.

The first time I realized Mike was high on cocaine was after Elvis, one of Adam's lieutenants, gave him an ounce while we were out on patrol. Mike called it a "Z"—short for ounce. I had no street knowledge of drugs, other than to smoke pot a few times in high school. What they taught us in the academy was mostly about heroin.

I didn't want coke in the car on duty. It bothered me how he was cutting a side deal with Adam's people in front of me, and I wasn't sharing in the profit—only the risk. Dowd tried to cool me off.

There was a huge difference between Adam Diaz's organization and La Compania. Adam had a direct line to Pablo Escobar in Colombia and dealt the best shit anywhere in the United States.

Because it was packaged in South America, cocaine was distributed using the metric system. Because the United States still used imperial weights and measures, Ken had to get a quick grasp on the metric system in order to understand the size and types of deals they would be making.

A kilo or a "key" is two-point-two pounds. That's 1,000 grams. A "Big Eight" is 125 grams. A "Z" or ounce weighs twenty-eight grams. An "8-Ball" is three-and-a-half grams. The smallest unit being packaged was a gram. Those are the normal selling points. At that time your average drug user is buying one gram for anywhere from seventy-five to one hundred dollars depending on quality and the greed of the selling dealer. Sometimes a few users would pool their money and purchase an "8-Ball" for $150.

Mike and I got the coke for free so everything was pure profit. When we started buying the coke later on, depending on the quantity we would spend anywhere from $600 for an ounce to $16,000 for a key of pure coke. And what we had tested 94 percent pure cocaine.

At that purity rate I was able to "step on it," "cut it," or "whack it" quite a bit.

When I cut coke, I used inositol, a compound which is now used in energy drinks. I read how it increased the "feel good" chemicals in the brain like serotonin and norepinephrine. It also gave a slight burning effect when snorted. I'd buy 250 grams at a health food store for twenty dollars.

Every gram I sold was 50 percent inositol and 50 percent cocaine. I made thirty-seven dollars and fifty cents for every half gram of inositol when I sold a gram for seventy-five dollars. That's $18,750 gross on the inositol jar that I would buy for twenty dollars. Add to that the profit from the cocaine you can understand why guys like Adam and Chelo were driving around in Porsches and Jags with Rolexes and hot girls.

When it came to extravagance, Chelo was among the most blatant drug dealers East New York had ever seen. By some measures he was making $200,000 a week at just two corners. He spent the money on leather pants, fur wraps, snake-skin shoes, and an array of weapons including Uzis and shotguns that were effective for settling just about any business dispute.

Adam Diaz, on the other hand, was making hundreds of millions of dollars a year. At its height, Adam's organization rivaled Fortune 100 companies for the sheer amount of business they were doing.

Adam and his crew were getting into the best night clubs, wearing the finest jewelry, and buying as many cars and as much real estate as they could get their hands on. In many ways Adam was the Tony Montana of East New York. But Adam was much smarter than his fictional counterpart and much more willing to make deals that benefited him and his partners. Adam also had a knack for staying out of and away from trouble. Having cops on his payroll who provided bullet-proof vests, guns, and other equipment made Adam untouchable.

He was on no one's radar. Adam was a legend among his peers—well-liked, clever, and astute.

Ken sensed that.

    I knew what the dealers were driving.
    I was driving a Chevy Chevette when I
    first partnered with Dowd. I thought,
    hell, drug dealing will pay real well
    once I get started.

International jewel heist mastermind Pavle Stanimirovic was more than familiar with the entire scene as he lived, played, and committed elaborate thefts, including thefts of drugs and drug money from dealers.

"When Mikey didn't get caught, he was hooked," said Pavle. "It was like an Atlantic City casino jackpot that pays every time you play a slot machine. Mikey D was off to the races. These races had consequences. But, he avoided them at first. He made many bad cases stick. He did what he needed to do.

"Like, who am I to judge? I would have done the same," said Pavle. "That was easy money. Pull off a ten-year run, stay above ground, and you are a multi-millionaire. Having Mike and Ken on his team gave Adam unparalleled power in East New York."

Despite the extra income of $8,000 a week, Mike and Ken wanted more.

One night on patrol Mike and Ken rolled up to Adam's place on Atlantic. He hit the siren for a second, and Adam's guy Elvis came out. He leaned on the driver's side window. Mike wanted an ounce.

"Hey give me a 'Z,'" Mike said, using the street slang to describe an ounce. Elvis ran into the shop for a second and returned with the blow. No charge.

After Mike got coke from Adam's guy Elvis, he told me to stop by his house later and he would give me some. I knew a bunch of casual coke users so I took one with me intending to sell him what Dowd would give me. I drove to Dowd's house in Brentwood with my buddy.

So I get to Mike's place in Brentwood around 8:00 p.m. He invites us in, offers us a drink, but I just want to get down to the deal and go back home. I told Dori I would only be gone an hour or so. Here she was, a young wife and a new mother. I'm working crazy hours as a cop. Now, on top of that, I'm running out at night to do coke deals. She had no clue.

We go into a back bedroom. It is dimly lit, and on the floor Dowd has a small scale with Elvis's ounce of coke next to it. Mike normally talked a lot, but he was high and he was yapping non-stop, sweating profusely, eyes dilated, and all the classic symptoms. He starts measuring out coke for me, but he couldn't stop his hands from shaking. Meanwhile my buddy's eyes are lit up. Here he is a casual coke user who has never seen more than a few grams staring at an uncut ounce rock busted off a key.

Mike had a few lines laid out, and he was ready to sample them. I thought he was going to have a heart attack right there in front of me.

"Yo! What the fuck are you doing?" I screamed at him.

"What?" Mike replied in a hushed voice with his hand motioning downward so his wife wouldn't hear the commotion.

"Do me a favor, lay off this shit. Please? Will ya?" I said. "This is to make money! Not for you to put up your nose."

"Don't worry about it," Mike replied before bending over and snorting up a line of the white powder he had laid out on the mirror.

When we got out of there, I asked my buddy about the coke.

"How was it?'"

"Fucking great! I'd definitely buy this from you."

It was at that moment Ken became a cocaine dealer on Long Island.

# CHAPTER 17. LAWYERS, GUNS, AND MONEY

In the mid-1980s and into the early '90s, the five-square miles encompassed by the Seven Five might as well have been Dresden in 1945. There was no resemblance to a gleaming American metropolis. Buildings dissolved into brick piles. Store fronts were abandoned, burned out, and tagged from top to bottom. Broken glass was common in alleys populated by zombies intent on that next five-dollar fix.

East New York's insatiable appetite for rock cocaine fueled all sorts of deadly behaviors. In the radio cars on patrol, cops handled one call after another. Some nights 200 calls backed up. Murder, rape, robbery, guns, drugs, shit on every corner. Some of it was expected. Some of the shit came out of nowhere. If the cops weren't going to stem the flow of crime like they thought when they came out of the academy they needed to know how to survive on the streets. Survival was key.

New York in 1986 and 1987 was also beset by racial tension. In December 1986 three black teenagers were confronted by an angry white mob in Howard Beach, Queens. The confrontation proved deadly; one of the teens was killed when he tried to escape his attacker and ran into the street. The young man was struck by a car and killed.

Two days after Christmas, the Rev. Al Sharpton led a protest march in the neighborhood. He and other members of his group accused the NYPD of covering up the worst racial aspects of the crime and demanded that Commissioner Benjamin Ward be held accountable.

Ultimately Governor Mario Cuomo stepped in and put special prosecutor Charles Hynes on the case. Hynes was the man largely responsible for putting away the thirteen Buddy Boys cops involved in the Seven Seven drug scandal. He had a reputation for being tough but fair.

Cuomo's move to placate Sharpton and other community organizers demanding justice in Queens had the unintended consequence of spreading Hynes too thin. Hynes's absence as the watchman over NYPD, combined with Ward's absolute unwillingness to expose the NYPD to more scandal, left neighborhoods like East New York vulnerable to drug crime and corruption. It allowed cops like Dowd and Eurell to take the skills they learned in the academy and put them to use as enforcers, couriers, and dealers.

On the streets of East New York in 1986, 1987, and 1988, those were powerful skills to have. They may have even saved Kenny's life.

Cops learn to read body language. They know how a man walks when he's carrying a gun. They know how the pupils of drug suspects are dilated or constricted. They know when someone's dealing or when someone's stealing. Dowd and Ken were taking money from East New York's worst dealers, but with all the other shit happening to the NYPD, they were flying under the radar and following a set of rules that only applied to the street. The partners, who had a lot in common—on and off the job—weren't afraid of being busted.

There were other on-the-job hazards that could cause trouble. And, those hazards were multiplied when your business partners were stone-cold killers.

```
While doing paperwork in a patrol car
I spotted two teenage boys—young men
maybe. They were eighteen or nineteen.
I noticed they were walking towards us.
One had a pocketbook in his hand and
```

was swinging it around like a plane propeller. You would think if you're dirty and saw cops you would walk in the opposite direction. They didn't.

I could see the pocketbook was weighted down with something. They continued walking towards us in the patrol car. When they got too close, I jumped out. I grabbed the kid with the pocketbook by the neck and slammed him face down onto the hood of the patrol car.

I grabbed the pocketbook out of his hands and threw him away from me. I immediately confirmed he had a gun.

"Get the fuck out of here," I yelled at the kid as he ran away. The kid was halfway down the block before I even got the words out of my mouth.

La Compania had dropped a lot of bodies in the Seven Five, and there was very little preventing the gang from adding a cop or two to the roll call. They'd nearly done that already: Members of Chelo's crew once engaged in a high-speed pursuit with homicide cops from the Seven Five.

The cops were in a van doing a routine surveillance when they got made. A group of bad guys approached the van with heavy-duty weapons and every intent of killing the cops inside. Instead, the detectives took off and—at high speeds—were chased back to the precinct house by the bad guys.

So it was a fact: Chelo didn't think twice about killing. He killed for sport, and he hired guys to kill for him when running the drug business began to interfere with doing the killing himself. Oddly enough, some of the guns that were on the street—even those that could be used to kill cops or innocent civilians, were put there by Dowd and Eurell.

> During our partnership, Dowd and I supplied dealers with: .357 Magnums, sawed-off shotguns, 9 mms, and .25 Ravens. And with all that Dowd and I were doing back then, we hardly ever got in any trouble at all. The worst was we lost four hours vacation time each.

The lost time came after a visit to Perez's shop. By this time Trimboli had his suspicions about what was happening at Auto Sound City and had once—recklessly—entered the place when a dope deal was in progress. One of Trimboli's co-workers had the place under surveillance when Ken and Mike arrived in uniform.

> On our meal hour we decided to stop by Perez's new radio shop to eat and pick up our weekly pay off. After around forty minutes we walked back out to the patrol car. The money was stuffed down Dowd's pants. Waiting outside was an Integrity Control Officer, but he didn't approach us when we left Perez's shop with the money. Instead he called us into his office a few days later. He wanted to know why Dowd and I were inside Baron's shop for so long.
> "We were on meal break," Dowd explained.

The ICO's write up noted Ken and Dowd parked their patrol car on the sidewalk and were not wearing hats.

Somehow he missed the bulge in Dowd's pants. The partners were docked four hours of vacation for their petty infractions. Dowd took the reprimand in stride.

"Four hours vacation time in trade for eight grand, that's not too bad, eh Ken?"

While the partners were getting an education in cocaine, they knew little about heroin, but it didn't prevent them from trying to score when opportunities arose.

One chance to snag heroin came when the partners responded to a report of shots fired in another sector of the 75th Precinct. Ken and Mike arrived first. They knew that the unusual call of shots fired in a residential neighborhood, not in their sector, offered an opportunity to grab money and drugs.

```
    As we approach the front door we can
see there is a DOA shot in the head.
He's in a pool of blood sort of blocking
the doorway. We jump over the body and
enter. There are voices coming from
upstairs. We don't see anyone.
    "Help us! Please help us!"
    All that's running through my head is
the question: Are these perps or victims?
    "Police! Police! Don't move!"
    We quickly scan and clear the ground
floor.
    "We're up here. Help us!"
```

The cops experienced an adrenaline rush that flowed from the absolute uncertainty of the situation.

```
    Other units are starting to arrive on
the scene, and the guys from Anti-Crime
```

attempt to take over. Dowd and I go on a search of the house knowing the victim was most surely killed for drugs.

In the front upstairs room we find an open safe. The safe is empty from what I see, but Dowd was alone in the room for a minute. That's all it takes for him to shove money down his pants. With the house filling up with other cops I watch the door while Dowd re-ransacks the rest of the bedroom with me there. We find an ounce or two of heroin, a 9 mm, and a MAC 10. Dowd puts the heroin in a paper lunch bag.

Just then one of the Anti-Crime cops tries to enter the space.

"We got this room," I tell him.

The good cop just backed out as I closed the door in his face. He clearly knew what we were doing, so we left him the guns and he never said anything. The cop who took the guns later retired as a hero detective.

Now a sergeant arrives.

"What's going on here?" he asked.

Dowd didn't have enough time to stuff the paper bag of heroin down his pants so he put it down on top of a garbage can at the top of the stairwell. Ken told his boss they were leaving the scene to get back to work. Their sergeant said that was a good plan as there were several calls for service that needed to be cleared.

The men then pulled a slight-of-hand, grabbing the heroin through a banister behind the boss's back.

"You're fucked up; you took that right in front of the

boss!" Ken said as they left.

"That idiot doesn't know shit," Dowd replied. "He was happy you told him we're picking up a job."

Instead of going to work, Mike and Ken headed to Auto Sound City. At Perez's shop, Ken and Mike met a man nicknamed "Gordo." He earned the nickname for obvious reasons. Gordo cut up the heroin, packaged it, and put it on the street. Ken and Mike got a small percentage, but it wasn't anywhere what they were making in the cocaine trade.

Ken and Dowd might as well have been full-time employees of the Diaz organization. They surveilled sales points and made specific recommendations about how Diaz's people could avoid the scrutiny of cops and robbers alike.

Some of the advice was common sense. Since East New York was a complete disaster, the cops advised Adam that his high-end customers might be at risk driving new Porsches and Mercedes Benzes into the neighborhood. Want to draw attention to yourself and your drug sales operation in the heart of East New York? Let rich guys come by in fancy cars and park right in front of your spot. Talk about your dead giveaways.

In return for the good and timely advice, Adam was generous, respectful, and always paid on time.

In spite of all the good advice, Diaz's first sales outlet on New Lots Avenue attracted some attention. Once when Eurell and Dowd were cruising by the shop they spotted a plainclothes cop tossing a suspect's car in the middle of the street. The partners offered their assistance. As uniformed cops they explained it would keep the scene secure and allow the detective to continue his work. Standing there in the middle of the street, Ken devised a plan to get rid of the officer.

Earlier in the week, Adam pointed out to Dowd and Ken a location that was run by his nearest competitor. Ken told the plainclothes gang cop that he could make a huge drug bust and record a good arrest by going to an apartment around the corner where drugs were being sold.

They go to the location and make a quick drug arrest. My buddy is grateful and writes it up during the arrest that an anonymous source advised him of the drug location. Everybody is happy, street crime gets their arrest and overtime, the city gets a drug location closed, and Dowd and I quickly prove our value to Diaz.

Another way Ken and Mike helped Adam was by scouting new locations for him to expand his drug sales empire in East New York. One such spot was the store of Joe Arroyo, a businessman whom Ken had become friendly with during his career in the Seven Five. Ken put together a deal that helped Arroyo during a time when the city targeted Arroyo's bodega, which was on a block of empty lots and crumbling buildings, for an eminent domain takeover.

His building was the only building standing on the block. The city wanted to pay just $30,000 for the location. I recognized that I could help Joe get more money and solve Adam's problem at the same time. Mike and I connected Adam and Joe.

Adam bought the building for $60,000 cash. It was a win-win. The deal also introduced Adam, Mike, and Ken to Arroyo's son Jamie, who was known around the neighborhood as "Joe Adonis." As soon as he was paid, Arroyo caught up with Dowd, who was partnered for the day with a rookie. Arroyo passed Dowd two envelopes stuffed with cash as a way of saying thank you for putting together the deal with Adam.

Mike got on the radio and hailed Ken, who was driving a sergeant that afternoon. Dowd wanted to meet up then and there. When the two former partners caught up with one another, Ken was still in the patrol car with the sergeant. It didn't matter to Dowd who passed him the cash-filled envelope.

"Oh is this the invitation to the party he was telling us about?" Ken asked Dowd.

Mike let out a high-pitched cackle that was part giggle and part laugh.

"Yeah, yeah, the party."

Neither the sergeant paired with Ken nor the rookie paired up with Dowd ever caught on. Ken thinks they were too stupid to see what was going on right under their noses.

Now that he had a new building, Adam and his people set about renovating the place. Diaz and his people built some cocaine sales renovations into the building. The renovations actually made the operation much safer—and way less likely to be robbed. Essentially the system kept the customers, their cash, and the drugs from being in the same place at the same time.

A good thing can't last forever. And eventually Ken and Mike told Adam he would have to move again. But they had a spot in mind—Baron Perez's original Auto Sound City location on Atlantic and Van Siclan. The location paired nicely with a bodega and third floor apartment across the street. More security systems could be enacted—again with the goal of keeping the customers, the drugs, and the dough from all being in one place at one time. One added benefit was the amount of parking available in the lot of the McDonald's next door to the former stereo shop.

Another task assigned to Ken and Mike was disruption. Essentially Adam wanted the officers to make it hard for any other dope dealers who wanted to compete with him. Occasionally this required muscle and manpower. Sometimes they'd hire Guevara and Dowd's brother Robert, who was a cop in the 105th Precinct.

I was in court one day when Dowd was guarding a female prisoner in the hospital. He starts smooth-talking her and learns she was arrested when detectives doing a door-to-door search for a missing person stumbled upon her apartment after a recent drug delivery. Everyone in the apartment was arrested, but the detectives missed all the money in the apartment, which was hidden in a bathroom ceiling tile.

Mike and I arranged to break-in with Chickie's help. But by the time we arrived, the money was gone. Either the detectives grabbed it or the prisoner was lying. Who knows? Dowd might have stolen the money when Chickie and I had our backs turned.

More often than not the group scored. But there were times when they missed money too.

During a fire at a first floor apartment that started in a kitchen, Dowd told me, "There's money here." Mike could have been a super cop if he did the right

157

things. After the fire was put out by the fire department, whose members were later accused by the owner of stealing jewelry, Dowd and I were waiting to secure the location or for the owner to return to the scene so I thought. Mike wanted me to search the kitchen with him.

The kitchen was destroyed and filled with soot and smoke. I was complaining about the smoke and not being able to breathe. The floor was weakened and damaged by the fire and water. Dowd unwillingly agreed to wait outside without searching the kitchen. Eventually the owner shows up.

"Do you have any money or valuables that you want to remove? " Dowd asked.

"My sons have some money in the kitchen." he answered.

Dowd flashed me a look that could kill.

The owner went inside and removed four coffee cans filled with hundred dollar bills. We missed about fifty thousand dollars. Dowd was sick to his stomach.

For the remainder of the day Dowd, in a whiny high-pitched wail, mocked Ken, "The smoke, the smoke I can't breathe."

Sometimes other cops got the money before we could. At one call complaining about drug sales, we arrived with two back-up units. I spotted about $5,000 hidden in a crack in the basement wall. I was reluctant to take it, fearing the other cops would see me and say something. So I tell Mike where I saw it, figuring he'd have no problem grabbing it.

Unfortunately, two minutes later when I attempted to show Mike, it was gone, another cop on the scene had already pocketed it.

Dowd's cocaine use began to spiral out of control. He was using consistently and found himself in dangerous situations. Yet, his supervisors saw him as an exemplary cop.

"This officer has excellent street knowledge: relates well with his peers and is empathetic to the community," a 1987 performance review noted. "This officer could excel within the New York City Police Department and easily become a role model for others to emulate if he maximized his inner drive to fulfill job responsibilities to the fullest. Must improve attendance and arrest activity. Good career potential."

Out of sight of his superiors, Dowd constantly pushed the boundaries. At a party hosted by Baron Perez, Mike got into a shouting match and a fight with another guest. He wound up getting stabbed.

Robert Dowd and I rushed Mike to the local hospital where we were friendly with the Emergency Room staff but not before Robert and I beat the shit out of the stabber. As the happy event turned into a brawl, the cops from our own precinct showed up and told us to take off before any bosses arrived.

Dowd was treated for his injury, and the hospital staff agreed to cover up the incident by not filing any reports or paperwork.

The event didn't prevent Dowd from starting trouble elsewhere. His attitude turned an altercation at a Nassau County bar into a brawl.

Mike, myself, and this little guy Tommy Risorto were drinking in a bar full of locals. I could feel the air getting tense. Dowd was high and obnoxious, and Tommy was flexing his beer muscles.

I go use the restroom figuring we could leave when I came back out. As I walk over to the bar, bam! I get hit in the head from behind with a glass pitcher. All I saw were stars. I immediately turn around and bear hug the guy who hit me slamming us both hard onto the barroom floor. I'm not sure what happened next, but eventually I was able to brush myself off and walk out of the bar. Dowd was waiting outside. The guy who hit me and the bar's glass window were both gone.

At this point I'm bleeding like a stuck pig. We jump in Dowd's car and remember he's got blow in the trunk. The bartender must have called the Nassau County cops because we didn't get far before they pulled us over with lights and sirens. The Nassau cops were told we shot out the front window of the bar. So Dowd and I immediately identify ourselves as police officers. They take Dowd's gun and start smelling it to see if it was fired.

I'm yelling at the cops, "Sometimes

you win, sometimes you lose. This time
we lost!

"Look at my head! They threw a fucking
barstool at the window!"

Professional courtesy took over. They
let us leave without taking any further
information from us. Then they tell us
to be safe on the drive home and to get
my head treated. My poor wife. Now I'm
waking her at four in the morning so
she can drive me to the hospital for
stitches. It took twelve to close the
gash in my head.

It was only a matter of time before the whole shit show
would fall apart. Kenny was blinded by the easy money, and
Mike was using cocaine with abandon. Not only that, he was
selling on the side.

Even so, Dowd had enough money left over to buy a
new red Corvette with a white top and paid cash for it. The
very next day he started driving the Corvette to work. If that
wasn't bad enough, he was parking it in the bosses' spots.

Kenny was pissed at Dowd's recklessness. Dowd told
him he worried too much. The more people that knew what
they were doing, the better, was Dowd's motto. It fit in with
the department's absolute inability to take action.

All the while, the FIAU guy Trimboli was watching, but
he was unable to get the bosses to buy into his theory that
Dowd was a criminal with a badge. He was getting a lot of
information from Joe Adonis, who didn't really know shit
about the operation, but it kept Trimboli on the trail of Dowd
and Eurell and—as long as he was snitching—kept Adonis
out of Central Booking.

Ken did everything he could to fly under the radar.

"I didn't want anyone to ever know what we were doing," Ken said.

Dowd's risk taking got even more brazen.

We were working a midnight shift. Around two or three in the morning there is a black female walking down the sidewalk. Dowd pulls over and tells her to get in. At first I thought he was going to question her about drug locations we could hit. As soon as she got in the car, Dowd started driving away.

"What are we doing?" I asked.

"Don't worry about it," Dowd replied.

The girl smelled foul. I realized she was a prostitute. She must have been out for the last twelve hours fucking and sucking every guy in East New York. She smelled horrendous. Dowd drives down to The Pool and parks. He takes off his gunbelt and jumps in the back with her. They start going at it. He stops and throws a condom into the front telling me to join him. I was so repulsed I had to lie to him and tell him I had a blowjob before I came to work.

The coke was turning Dowd into a sex-obsessed maniac. Not only did he have a wife at home, he had a girlfriend in the precinct house. And, in his personal life, he was making dangerous moves.

"What if they piss test you?" Ken asked.

"So fucking what?"

Dowd may have been fucked up, but he was far from delusional about himself and his own role. Once Michael

Dowd was asked whether he considered himself to be a cop or a drug dealer, he replied that he was "both." The same interviewer asked Dowd whether he worked for the NYPD or Pablo Escobar's Colombian cocaine cartel and Dowd answered, "I guess I'd have to say the drug traffickers."

By early 1988, although the Internal Affairs investigators could get nothing on him or members of his crew, Dowd was clearly a crook—not a cop. He and Ken proved their loyalties when on February 6, 1988, dispatch reported a man with a machine gun at an address that Mike and Ken knew as Diaz's primary sales location. The partners arrived at the scene first, and Elvis, Diaz's lieutenant, was waiting for them.

"I've been robbed," Elvis said.

"What the fuck? What did they get?" the cops asked. "Who was it?"

"It was Franklin and Coke. They took kilos, cash, and the .357 Magnum you gave me. Fuck."

Franklin was a stickup man, who specialized in taking off cocaine dealers. Coke was his partner. After ripping off Adam's guy Elvis, Franklin and Coke took off eastbound on Atlantic in a blue Cadillac.

As other cops from the Seven Five began to arrive at the scene, Ken and Mike realized they had work to do for Adam—protect the rest of Adam's stash and catch the sons-of-bitches.

# CHAPTER 18. FRANKLIN AND COKE

After establishing that no one was actually shot, Ken and Mike worked out a plan to keep Adam's coke and money away from nosy detectives.

"Elvis, just advise the officers that the first floor bodega was robbed. Don't tell them anything else," Ken said as he and Dowd left the scene to search for Franklin and Coke.

Sometime later a call comes over the radio. An officer at the scene arrested two of Adam's people for possession of drugs and guns.

"This was a shitstorm for us," Ken said. "It was a major financial blow to Adam, and that meant lost money for us."

For three days Dowd and Ken scoured the Seven Five looking for Franklin. He was going to be turned over to the Diaz organization. No questions asked.

The partners waited outside a coffee shop on New Lots Avenue, where they believed Franklin would turn up. Eventually he did. He owned the place.

"We pulled over his car as he drove away in broad daylight. Dowd gave Franklin numerous automobile summons, which he never filed with the police department. The purpose was to get Franklin's verified address."

That was the end of Franklin. Sometime after that traffic stop, the stickup man disappeared.

"All I know is that Franklin has not been heard from since," Kenny said. "He was carried as a missing persons case for years."

His coffee shop was quickly shuttered and abandoned like every other building in the Seven Five.

"Let's just say he's gone," Adam said when interviewed.

"You won't be hearing from Franklin."

Eventually Franklin was reported missing. Ken thinks he disappeared due to a deportation. He's never come forward.

As for Coke?

Diaz simply said, "He's not coming back."

For certain, the Diaz organization's business was slowed by the robbery and the subsequent arrest of his employees and other key figures within the organization.

Payments to Ken and Mike began to taper off, but they still had fun.

We spent money as fast as it came in; we were out every night, bought homes, cars, clothes, furniture, and gambled. There were limo trips we took to Atlantic City. When we went to restaurants the $400 to $500 bills were paid with fives and tens. On precinct bus trips to Atlantic City, where most officers would bring $200, Dowd and I would bring $5,000 each.

During one trip to Atlantic City we stopped in a stretch limo at Baron's new shop to pick up our weekly payoff from Diaz. While we were there, other 75th Precinct officers working in the neighborhood spotted the big classy limo in the drug-infested neighborhood.

Dowd wanted to talk to Baron. I stayed in the car with Chickie and some girls who came along for the ride. Dowd got out and entered Baron's shop. The beat cops thought something was up. But only for a minute.

"Hey boys!" Dowd shouted at the men in their patrol car.

And, that was enough to let them know the limo was okay and so were its passengers. The cops who thought they were on to something instead went on to take care of other business.

Even though we had the money to go to Atlantic City and have fun. There was always work to do—and it wasn't only providing protection for Adam.

Dowd and I did more than our share of police work. In fact we handled more jobs than other units because we were always "looking." Not for an arrest or summons, but for drugs and money. We probably took more guns off the street than the rest of our squad combined; unfortunately we sent all the guns back onto the streets. We were both extremely experienced and never needed to tie up the bosses with questions about how to handle routine situations.

This also allowed us freedom. We were in great shape physically and never called for backup from other units. We were usually the first to arrive when others called for backup.

The Dowd-Eurell partnership swung into pro-active action when a plainclothes transit cop was murdered responding to a drug stick-up on Pitkin Avenue.

According to official accounts, Officer Robert Venable was shot and killed as he and five other officers attempted to make an arrest of two heavily armed men at an abandoned building at 2569 Pitkin Avenue in Brooklyn.

Venable and two other cops were bringing several

prisoners to Brooklyn's Central Booking when they were approached by several citizens who were concerned about men with guns who had just appeared in the neighborhood. As the officers approached the scene, Venable was shot.

The guy who shot Venable had been out of prison and on parole for forty-two days. Venable left behind an eight-year-old daughter, grieving parents, and shocked friends.

Ken and Mike heard the 10-13 (officer needs assistance) in their patrol car.

"Shots fired! Shots fired!"

They arrived in under a minute, the first unit on the scene, and took fire. Even so, Dowd, Eurell, and one of Venable's comrades carried the severely wounded officer to Ken's patrol car.

> He was bleeding profusely from a very large head wound. The housing officer and I were getting him into the backseat as fast as we could while Dowd ran around to the driver's seat so we could get to the hospital. I remember we had a difficult time getting Venable's feet completely into the car because he was so big. Dowd started to drive away before we could even get the door closed.

Ken took to the radio and ordered dispatch to notify Brookdale Hospital that he and Dowd would be arriving with an officer who was shot in the head.

> Then I proceeded to give the route we were taking, hoping other units would shut down some intersections while Mike raced us through the neighborhood at

lightning speed.

Arriving at the hospital I expected a full medical team to be waiting for us. I don't know the reason, but absolutely nothing, nobody was there waiting. Either we got there too fast or central failed to make the notification. We grabbed a gurney, put Officer Venable's lifeless body on it, and rolled him inside while yelling for help that we have an officer shot. Hospital staff then took over for us.

Eventually Dowd and Eurell returned to the scene. They were covered in Venable's blood. The stickup men were pinned down. Brass was there, so was the press.

Instead of sending Dowd and I to the station house to be questioned by the detectives or the hospital to see if we needed mental or physical treatment, the bosses demanded to know why we weren't wearing our fucking hats. Obviously because the press is on the scene they were concerned about appearances, but give me a fucking break, this wasn't mid-town Manhattan, it was the Land of Fuck.

The shit on the streets was bad following Venable's murder. Mike and Ken decided to buy bigger guns to protect themselves from fools who would kill cops. These were going to be back-up pieces. Ken bought a dull black finish 9 mm. Mike bought the same gun, except it was flashy and all chrome. They carried them on-duty as back-up weapons from then on.

About two weeks later a sergeant in the precinct approached me and told me Officer Venable was a relative. He had heard what we did, and he thanked me for taking care of the wounded officer and thanked us for rushing him to the hospital.

The last bit of real action Ken and Mike saw was an incident that nearly became a fatal officer involved shooting.

It seemed Dowd and I got along better with the street element than we did other officers. While I was taking a report for an automobile accident, people started yelling there was a man with a gun down the block. Thank goodness we were both experienced because I know other cops would have shot this guy.

As we drive up to the scene, sure enough there's a male Hispanic in the middle of the street pointing an automatic handgun at two male blacks. Mike and I jump out of the patrol car standing behind the doors and point our guns at the man with the gun. He's not saying a fucking word.

The two black men are yelling at me and Mike, "Shoot him! Shoot him! He's got a gun!"

We began to yell. "Don't move! Drop the fucking gun! Drop the gun!"

After what seemed like an eternity, the man with the gun doesn't drop the gun like he's ordered, but he starts moving the gun downward toward his side and reaching behind his back with his other hand. We would have been justified killing this guy but we held off just a second more, suddenly the gunman pulls out a black shield case flipping it open and states he's an undercover narcotics officer.

Really? Pulling something black from behind your back? Suspects have been shot multiple times for far, far less in recent years. We got lucky this time. Imagine how it would have looked if we shot an undercover narc.

The two perps knew they were in trouble. The undercover officer had witnessed them making a drug buy but was waiting for his backup so he didn't want to reveal his identity in the street. The backup team finally arrived as we were now holding down the suspects. The undercover officer didn't even thank us for not shooting him or at the least for capturing his perps.

About two months later while I was in the neighborhood off-duty and having a beer with a neighborhood bodega owner, a guy approached me asking if I remembered him. When I said that I didn't know who he was, he placed his hand around his own neck which is how I took him down for the undercover.

"You remember me now?" the man asked. "You and your partner are alright. That

```
asshole cop wanted to kill us. I just
want to thank you."
   We then had a beer together.
```

Kenny and Mike didn't know it, but Trimboli and the Internal Affairs clowns weren't the only cops eyeing them. The federal Drug Enforcement Agency had been keeping track of their activity for several months.

During the year and a half the men were partners, DEA agents linked them to:

• Stealing heroin and cocaine from a murder/crime scene

• Stealing money from a burglary crime scene by having the victim identify where her mother kept money, which had not been stolen in the initial burglary

• Using excessive force on prisoners and civilians

• Riding shotgun with drug traffickers to protect transportation of drugs and money

• Using cocaine and alcohol on duty

• Purchasing and selling ounce to kilogram quantities of cocaine

Higher ups were suspicious but worried that if they acted against Dowd and Eurell it would expose the department to questions about leadership and calls for reform from citizens who had no idea how to run a police department in New York City in the 1980s.

Even so, a reckoning was at hand. In early summer of 1988, Dowd was called in to take a drug test. Rather than show up, he checked himself into "The Farm" an alcohol treatment program run by the department, which allowed officers to dry out.

The brass, assuming something was up, started fucking with Eurell. As a result, Ken got stuck with shit duty—sitting on dead bodies and walking foot posts on the midnight shift.

> I'd go in, look at the roll call and see they'd have me alone on fucking Pitkin and Pine, just a few blocks east of where Venable got shot. This was one of the most dangerous drug locations in the precinct for any tour, and I was there alone on a midnight. In the old days I'd just sleep in the precinct lounge, but I knew they were looking to fuck me and I just dealt with it. Someone really had it in for me.

Ken was alert but not intimidated and stopped regularly carrying the back-up piece. Intimidation wasn't a hallmark of Dowd's crew. All anyone had to do was look at Walter Yurkiw, the most intimidating presence in the precinct house or on the street.

# CHAPTER 19. THE R & T
# GROCERY STORE ROBBERY

No one who ever saw Walter Yurkiw ever forgot him. At six-five, 290, the big, mean redhead was part of Dowd's crew since coming over to the Seven Five in 1986. Yurkiw drank on the job, snorted coke like a rock star, and when he was bored, Yurkiw beat suspects for fun.

It goes without saying that Yurkiw was not a guy to be fucked with under any circumstances. Maybe he sensed he was different. Maybe he knew he could get away with it. Whatever drove Big Walter, one thing would become certain, his career as a cop was corrupt nearly from day one.

In his unpublished memoir, portions of which have been posted on Twitter, Yurkiw said the first time he took money from a crime scene was as a rookie in the 103rd Precinct in Queens. His life of crime escalated from there.

Unlike Dowd and Eurell, who lived out in the comfortable Long Island suburbs, Walter shacked up with a dishwater blonde badge bunny who believed she could change him. He called a brownstone walk-up on a tree-lined and run-down section of Bay Street in Bensonhurst his home.

Walter typically defied convention. And he was unafraid to shit where he ate. When he was bad, which was most of the time, Yurkiw hung out in the Seven Five and, like Chickie Guevara, Yurkiw was a valued member of Dowd's crew.

In '86, '87, and '88, cops like Dowd and Yurkiw fashioned a new type of corruption. It generated huge paydays and lifestyles that rivaled those of the rich and famous. These were not the good guys that ran toward danger like those who made the ultimate sacrifice in the World Trade Center on 9/11. These were thugs, punks, lowlifes, and opportunists. As one investigator described it, Mike Dowd's crew was "walking around with lead-lined gloves and riding shotgun for organized crime."

Back in the 1970s, when Frank Serpico exposed deep-seated NYPD corruption in testimony before the Knapp Commission, the country learned what it meant to be a meat-eater in the department. Essentially a meat-eater was a cop who exploited his position for financial gain—taking payoffs to ignore low-level victimless crimes and vice like gambling or prostitution.

Dowd and his crew changed the definition forever, instead of taking money to look the other way during a street crime, they began competing with the criminals to commit street crimes themselves, that's how Michael Armstrong, the Knapp Commission's chief counsel saw it.

Yurkiw was one of fifteen members of Dowd's crew often regularly gathered at The Pool.

Dowd brought Yurkiw in the same way he worked Kenny. Dowd said each time he was assigned a new partner, he would deliberately "test" the partner's willingness to engage in corruption by getting the partner to commit some act of misconduct, like taking free cigarettes and booze from the bodegas or drinking on duty.

Dowd defined cops that saw things his way as "good." Cops that would turn away from corruption were "bad" in Dowd's twisted worldview.

Once Dowd knew a partner was "good," Mike would welcome the partner into an agreement to share the wealth of their misdeeds and protect each other from investigators or anyone who would stand in their way.

There were ways to work the scam. Cops in the Seven Five learned how to "sniff out" potentially profitable radio runs—and respond to those calls. Dowd was often the first to arrive on the scene and fill his pockets freely. Yurkiw was adept at it too.

Dowd's crew first became expert at shaking down street dealers. Basically cops in need of drugs or money would force dealers into an alleyway, behind a building, or some other secluded location, and steal as much as they could get their hands on. Dowd set shakedown goals of $300 to $500 a day—and more at Christmastime.

The key was to leave a drug dealer happy after one of the thefts. Happiness was key. If the dealer was happy he wouldn't complain and would quickly understand that shakedowns were like "taxes"—part of the cost of doing business.

Dowd's "good cops" were also good liars.

Investigators who were looking into NYPD corruption broke it down.

"Officers manufactured facts. For example, to justify an unlawful raid on a drug den where money or drugs were stolen, a common tale was that the officers entered the location in hot pursuit or on information from an unidentified informant. To justify unlawfully searching and arresting a street dealer from whom officers stole drugs or cash, a common tale was the person dropped a bag and ran as the officers approached," a report into Dowd and the Seven Five noted.

Beatings, something Yurkiw was famous for, were often covered up by the street cops and their immediate supervisors.

"A number of officers told us how they and others would insulate themselves from excessive force complaints simply by adding charges of 'resisting arrest' to an arrest report—a practice rarely questioned by supervisors. One officer reported how he and another officer chased and finally caught an individual who had run from his car after a traffic stop. While the officer was holding the individual, another officer struck the defendant in the head with his police radio. The officers then agreed upon a false story justifying their stop and search of the car and about the circumstances of the defendant's head injury," the investigators noted.

In one well-documented brutality incident, Brooklyn officers threatened to feed a suspect to a pack of pit bulls if he didn't reveal the location of his stash.

And as Dowd explained, there was a direct connection among cops that used excessive force and those that made street corner rip offs.

"The (police officers) that are taking money will more typically be the ones that are giving beatings," he said.

When drug money wasn't readily available on the streets, cops employed schemes, called "Collars-for-Dollars," that ratcheted up their overtime hours. Sometimes that meant just making up a crime. The scenarios that worked best to justify an arrest were:

(a) That you observed what appeared to be a drug transaction;

(b) You observed a bulge in the arrestee's waistband; or

(c) You were informed by a male black, unidentified at this time, that at that location, where the arrest was made, there were drug sales.

Cops saw the lies as a sort of way to balance the scales of justice, which they believed worked in favor of the drug dealers and stick-up men.

In the world of law enforcement, this behavior is known as "Noble Cause Corruption."

## Contemplating Corruption

It has been said that corruption is realistic. It deals with the real world and real relationships, while the laws, as written, are based on fantasy, repression, and denial of what human beings do and do not do.

True or not, there is a form of police corruption far more prevalent than the blatant criminality of Michael Dowd and Kenny Eurell. It's called "Noble Cause Corruption."

Noble Cause Corruption is committed in the name of good ends, and it is a corruption of police power when officers do bad things because they believe that the outcomes will be good.

A famous film example is the Orson Welles's classic *A Touch of Evil* in which a powerful police detective plants evidence to cinch a conviction. *Police Chief Magazine* devoted significant space to discussing this problem in their August 2016 edition. Examples of Noble Cause Corruption include planting or fabricating evidence, lying on reports or in court, and generally abusing police authority to make a charge stick.

"Officers do not normally define 'a bending of the rules for a greater good' as misconduct or as corruption," noted Thomas J. Martinelli, J.D., an adjunct professor at Wayne State University in Detroit, Michigan. "Rather, they rationalize that such behavior is part of the job description, in a utilitarian sense, to get the criminals off the streets, regardless of the means."

Cops don't often realize that when they violate the basic constitutional guidelines demanded by their profession, they become criminals themselves and expose their agency to horrific legal liability.

Unchecked, this behavior results in serious civil rights violations even in small towns. The city of Walla Walla, Washington, for example, was sued for $7 million—$1 million for each violation of the individual's civil rights. Cities carry insurance for such situations; no doubt Walla Walla's rates went up.

Beating people, best known simply as police brutality, is definitely against the law, but in New York City, cops routinely beat anyone with an attitude who crossed their path—especially in drug neighborhoods.

Beatings and shakedowns were a good way to break the corruption cherry, but there was far more money to be made in stickups. Dowd knew that if cops like Yurkiw and Guevara were involved, there would be no chance of anyone talking.

"Cops don't tell on cops," Dowd and other corrupt NYPD officers would say. "And if they did tell on them ... his career's ruined. He's going to be labeled as a rat. So if he's got fifteen more years to go on the job, he's going to be miserable because it follows you wherever you go. And he could be in a precinct—he's going to have nobody to work with. And chances are if it comes down to it, they're going to let him get hurt. You do not want to be labeled a rat. You will be the recipient of bad practical jokes, even things more serious than practical jokes. Then, to leave or request to leave the environment that you were in, wouldn't be the end of this labeling that you had. Phone calls would be made to wherever your final destination was in the department. Your name traveled with you. It was something you couldn't shake.

With money from Adam Diaz drying up, the R&T Grocery, a bodega at 923 Livonia, about two blocks southwest of the precinct house, was a perfect stick-up target for Dowd's crew.

The night air was cool on the evening of July 1, 1988. Sandwiched between deadly heat waves that gripped New York during the last week of June and again after Independence Day, temperatures had dropped into the fifties. The moon was nearly full but partly obscured as clouds formed in the night sky.

Like Adam's place on New Lots, R & T was a drug

supermarket. New York City Police Officer Walter Yurkiw's plan was to knock off the place before going in for his midnight shift. He brought along Officer Jeffrey Guzzo and former officer Henry "Chickie" Guevara. When the three burst into the store at 10:30 p.m. and told everyone to get on the floor, Walter was wearing a cap emblazoned with the letters NYPD.

After snatching $950, some fireworks, cigarettes, a six-pack of beers, and whatever dope was there, Yurkiw, Guzzo, and Guevara grabbed R & T's owner Braulio Lugo and forced him to lie on the floor of Walter's 1978 sky blue Lincoln Continental, while Guzzo held a 9 mm to Lugo's head. After fifteen minutes of aimlessly driving around the precinct, and nearly getting pulled over, Dowd's crew cut Lugo loose.

Lugo later told investigators that Walter was ready to kill the cops that nearly pulled them over. Fortunately for the patrol officers, they were dispatched to a shooting just before lighting up Walter's pimpmobile.

When he arrived at work for the midnight shift, Walter's car was a trash can. It was littered with crack pipes, drugs, drug scales, and cash. And Walter was lit up on a combination of coke, pot, and booze.

About the same time Walter clocked in, Lugo came down to the precinct house to report the robbery and spotted Walter's unique ride in the employee parking lot. Investigators arrested Yurkiw at his locker. When they tossed his car, they found everything Lugo said had been stolen.

No one accused Walter of being a genius.

The arrest caught the attention of Internal Affairs investigators and the Special Prosecutor's Office. A brief investigation led straight to Dowd and Bailey's Bar. It was Joe Adonis who led them there, telling investigators he had been in the bar on the night of the robbery with Dowd,

Yurkiw, Guzzo, and Guevara. The crew planned the stick up together.

Adonis had more. He told investigators with the US Attorney's office that Dowd worked for Adam Diaz and was clearing $4,000 a week to provide protection. The Feds passed their information onto the NYPD brass, and although it corroborated information investigators like Trimboli had already gathered, higher ups believed they didn't have enough good information to go after Dowd.

They did go after Chickie; they arrested him while he was tending bar at Bailey's. Ken was among the first to hear of the 2:00 a.m. arrest.

> I get a phone call from a guy who was at the bar with Chickie. My wife answers the phone, and the fucking guy says, "Annette let me talk to Kenny."
>
> Annette was a female cop in the Seven Five I was seeing at the time. The guy who called thought that was my wife's name, he probably had seen Annette and me together at Bailey's. So after I get off the phone, I need to deflect the Annette comment before I call Mike so we can go down to try and bail out Chickie.
>
> "Why did that loser call me Annette?" Dori asked.
>
> "He's fucking drunk, that's my new partner's name," I replied.
>
> Dori didn't buy it, but I didn't have time to argue.

Two weeks later detectives picked up Guzzo.

Yurkiw made bail following his arrest on the robbery, but

in August he got arrested again. This time he was making threats against his live-in girlfriend, a coke head.

In their reports about the alleged domestic violence incident NYPD Internal Affairs investigators would write, "She knew Yurkiw was a corrupt cop. She had seen him in his apartment with Dowd, Guzzo, and Guevara in possession of large quantities of cocaine and money laid out on the kitchen table."

In November, investigators were again talking to Walter's girlfriend, this time because he threatened to kill her. Now she had more to say.

She reported that Yurkiw told her that there was a group of twenty-five police officers in the 75th Precinct who were systematically robbing drug dealers and locations. She told investigators that she had seen 923 Livonia, which was the R & T, on a list of known drug locations in East New York. Walter kept the list in the glove box of the pimpmobile and had been going through the locations one-by-one since February 1987. She also told the cops that Yurkiw was taking stolen coke to Mike Dowd and Dowd's brother. The Dowd brothers, she said, were selling it on Long Island.

There was a hitch in what she was telling the Manhattan detectives from Internal Affairs. They didn't believe her.

In a report on interviews with the woman, investigators wrote that because she was an admitted drug abuser and Yurkiw's lover, "her credibility and allegiances" were suspect. That didn't keep cops from interviewing her every time she had a complaint. It also didn't prevent them from arresting Yurkiw and bringing him to the DA on suspicion of domestic violence counts.

The drama of the arrests scared the snot out of Ken.

```
    Guevara was in on a lot of what Dowd
and I had done. I had the feeling of
```

```
going to work every single day thinking
I was going to be arrested. I remember
walking into the back lot and looking at
the rear doors of the precinct thinking
IAD would be just inside waiting to put
cuffs on me.
```

They weren't.

Internal Affairs never initiated a single investigation into Dowd, and questions about his criminality "inevitably died a natural death." Cops began to wonder if Dowd was a snitch getting protection for his actions by turning in other officers. It was never clear.

# CHAPTER 20. A CALL FOR HELP

With Mike Dowd on The Farm "drying out," Ken slowly returned to regular police work.

I went opposite from Dowd, I turned around and went in the other direction. I was making about four arrests a month, and my overtime went way up. Slowly I was returned to work in a patrol car and taken off foot posts.

With nine years as a cop under his belt, Kenny was now the senior man in the Seven Five. But not for long. Fate intervened. The incident happened on July 10, 1988, during a swing shift tour of the Seven Five that almost saw Kenny get killed by a shitbird who was high on PCP, also known as "angel dust," and tried to take Ken's gun.

We were looking forward to getting off duty and going home after a very busy tour. As we approached the intersection of Fountain Avenue and Linden Boulevard a car goes flying by us on three tires and one rim. Sparks are flying out from behind the car, and as much as we want to end the night, we need to stop this car before the driver kills someone.
We pull in behind the car in the service lane on Linden and hit the lights. The guy just speeds up and starts going down side streets. He makes a turn onto

Dumont Avenue, loses control, and hits a telephone pole totaling the front end of the car.

Just like on TV, the car door flies open, and he's off and running down the street. I jump out of the patrol car and give chase through the construction sites in the city's refurbishing program. My partner starts backing the patrol car down the street following us. As we exit the construction site, the perp runs into a backyard. I'm still giving chase while my partner circles the block expecting us to come out on the other side.

In the backyard there was a big wood stockade fence. I have him trapped. Usually the perps realize there's no place to go and give up. This guy wasn't done. He turns towards me and lunges forward putting both his hands on the butt of my gun trying to take it out. I instinctively put my hands over his, pushing down, hopefully preventing him from pulling my gun out.

Had this been a few months earlier I probably would have pulled out my backup piece, a 9 mm, and shot him. They say your life flashes before your eyes during a near death experience. All I could think about while I was fighting for my life was my young son, Jimmy.

I can't believe I'm going to die alone in a dirty backyard in Brooklyn. So we're fighting back and forth, him trying to get the gun out of my holster, me keeping it in, and we lose our balance and start to fall. I put my right hand out to break the fall, and he comes down on top of me hyperextending my wrist, bending it all the way back. As soon as we hit, he jumps up and is off and running again.

I call a 10-85 for assistance, give the perp's direction of flight, and tell the responding units the description of the guy who just attempted to kill me. One unit finds the perp; one unit picks me up. He goes to the hospital and jail. I go to the hospital.

Ken briefly returned to light duty. On April 19, 1989, he was called into a meeting and brought along a union lawyer. Trimboli, from Internal Affairs, was there too.

"What is this about?" I asked Trimboli.

"It's nothing; don't worry about it," Trimboli said.

I get called into the room with my lawyer, and we sit down. The captain asks me about Bailey's Bar.

"It's just a bar that we stop at after work to drink and unwind," I tell him.

"What about 924 Blake Avenue?" was the captain's next question.

"924 Blake?"

"The bodega called Mr. Joes," the captain clarified asking about the business Dowd and I helped Adam Diaz acquire.

"Oh, he's a friend I've known for years. When I worked in the precinct I used to stop in once in a while for a beer."

At the outset of the meeting, Trimboli and the captain confiscated about eight of Ken's memo books. They covered the time he was partnered with Dowd. The memo books contained a lot of information that could have resulted in serious problems for Dowd and Eurell.

Dowd was telling me the story of a robbery he and Chickie did. On the backside of one of the memo pages, I wrote down the address and the name of the weed dealer they robbed.
Trimboli and the captain never saw it.

With that, the interview ended. Ken let out a sigh of relief when he was alone.

Five months later, on September 27, 1989, an application for my pension was submitted by the police commissioner on my behalf. I was officially retired on November, 30, 1989. I started drawing my pension. Under New York law, pensions due former public employees are treated as property in trust for the employee.
When I returned to the 75th Precinct to clear out my locker, other cops came over wishing me the best, saying they wanted to get a minor injury and retire as well. For a cop or firefighter, disability is a good thing if the injury isn't that serious. Walking with a minor limp or

not being able to hold and fire a gun is the end of a police officer's career, but if I was back in construction with my father I would still have to work. Different careers have different benefits. City employees like cops, firefighters, and even sanitation workers have excellent benefits.

This is what happens with an injury when you're a city employee. The medical review board, which consists of three professional doctors employed by the city, reviews the applicant's medical records. They then determine based on those records and on personal examinations they perform if the applicant will ever be at 100 percent again. Even if the applicant can recover to 99 percent, the city will opt to retire that employee with a small pension. The reason being is, if that employee ever returns to the street and (in a police officer's case) is involved in anyway where a civilian or even another officer is injured or killed, any civil attorney will sue the city for millions when they find out the officer wasn't 100 percent medically fit. It's strictly a numbers game for the bean counters.

Being at home all day and retired at a young age might sound like a fun thing, but it took a lot of getting used to. During the day my wife went back to work full time, and I took on the role of Mr. Mom. I would start looking for any excuse to get out of the house at night. I would meet my friends from the Seven Five in any bar after a swing shift. I returned for all the precinct parties. I began to go out with my younger brother John again. Something I hadn't done since my marriage in 1985. I was even going to gatherings in the Seven Three because my cousin was now an officer there. Last but not least, I started seeing Mike Dowd again.

When Dowd was reassigned in 1988 to NYPD's Whitestone Impound Yard in Queens, he worked a tow yard scam that netted kickbacks from tow truck companies, auto repair shops, and average citizens who bought him off. He also worked insurance scams that allowed his cronies to collect thousands from non-existent accidents and an assortment of fictional mishaps.

Then, reassigned to a foot beat in the 94th Precinct on the Brooklyn side of the East River, Dowd gathered information on a notorious dope dealer, then sold it to the man's rival. Among the information was the dope dealer's real name, date of birth, his wife's name, an address, and a telephone number.

Dowd by this time had been transferred to the 94th Precinct. His new partner, Tommy Mascia, went through the same routine with Dowd that I did. Mascia found himself without a partner because his last partner retired, and Dowd was soon in the patrol car with him. Dowd was now telling Mascia what he had done with me. Just as he told me what he did in

the past with Guevara and Dubois. Mascia
was soon involved in several crimes with
Dowd.

Mikey D had gone back to his old ways. Over the months
since Dowd and Kenny were split up, federal investigators,
watching from the shadows, chronicled a whole host of
criminal behavior by Dowd. Among their notes were some
significant bullet points about Dowd's activity. Among the
notes were instances of:
• Receiving kickbacks from tow truck companies for
referrals
• Receiving kickbacks from automobile repair shops for
referrals
• Making impound vehicles inoperable and then receiving
gratuities from owners for making the vehicles operable
• Creating false police reports to allow civilians to collect
insurance money in exchange for a kickback
• Providing drug traffickers with information from
police vouchers, including information about rivals like
their names, dates of birth, spouses' names, addresses, and
telephone numbers in exchange for money
• Stealing money from person or home of "dead on
arrival" victims
• Stealing money from drunks on the street
• Receiving money from drunken drivers in exchange for
not arresting them
Despite getting away with his betrayal of the badge, Ken,
now a stay-at-home dad, knew there was money in Dowd's
scheming and thought about ways he could get involved
again.

## CHAPTER 21. BACK IN THE GAME

Dowd was still selling cocaine and making very good money at it. I wasn't interested in dealing coke, but the prospect of making money stirred up those old feelings. On patrol Dowd was robbing the dead, removing items from burglary scenes, had a kickback scam with a towing company, and was picking up cocaine to sell on Long Island.

We discussed doing protection work for another drug organization. This was possible because Dowd was still in touch with Baron Perez. My cousin and his partner, Phil Carlucci, were willing to help out, but Perez didn't know any dealers in the Seven Three Precinct.

Jose "Chelo" Montalvo was dead. He had been gunned down in the Bronx. Adam was locked up.

So we went back to the Seven Five for names. Nothing came of it, and I didn't pursue it because my father in-law had passed away and left us a large sum of money. Between the inheritance, my pension, Dori back working full time, and a rental income, I was living well and didn't push for the scam.

Getting back into the game as a civilian on Long Island didn't afford the same protections for Ken as it did when

190

he wore a badge and went on patrol in the Seven Five with
Dowd and did rip and runs with Chickie and the crew. But
all good things come to an end. When Ken saw the light at
the end of the tunnel, he thought it meant he was going to
get out clean.

A few years after I left the NYPD I
started going to a number of Bayshore
bars and became good friends with people
who were harmless weekend cocaine users.
At the same time my cousin came to me with
an idea. My cousin's partner in the 73rd
Precinct dealt cocaine before becoming
a cop and wanted to start up again, but
he needed a supplier. They wanted to
know if I would be interested in pooling
together some money with them. I would
be required to make the connection with
Dowd for the cocaine then give it to my
cousin, who would in turn give it to his
partner. All the sales would be handled
by my cousin's partner, and we would
split the profits three ways.

I thought this sounded great. I
wouldn't have to lift a finger, and I
would be making a few extra dollars.

Dowd bought the coke and made deliveries
on his way home to Long Island from
Brooklyn.

At some point, because the cocaine
was so pure, I started to cut what
was intended for Carlucci's customers
and began selling it to my friends in
Bayshore. I was making twice the sales
on the same buy. At first I sold to my

cousin and Carlucci, and then to my friends in Bayshore. I quickly started to gain a reputation in Bayshore as a cocaine dealer. I was good at it. I gave my customers credit and free cocaine on their birthdays, which no one did.

My customer base grew very quickly. I went from being partners with my cousin and his partner to once again being partners with Dowd.

On Dowd's days off, I would go into Brooklyn with him. Dowd had a falling out with his dealer over money so the cocaine was now being bought through a Dominican named Ray. The routine was always the same. We beeped Ray to make sure he had the required amount on hand. The money would be dropped off at one location; then Dowd and I would pick it up from Ray at another location.

In between the money drop and coke pick-up, Dowd and I would hang around the Seven Five neighborhood bouncing between different bodegas and bars. The amount of cocaine we purchased varied, but was as much as a kilo sometimes. Dowd and I would divide the cocaine and then make some deliveries. We were partners in the buys, but we both had our own customers for sales. One of mine was a low level guy named Harry Vahjen, who I met through Patty Patwell, a bartender.

Vahjen wanted to be a big player. We went into the basement of a bar where Patwell worked. I gave Patwell a gram

of coke to give to Vahjen as a sample.
I told Vahjen to take his license out.
I looked at his name, told him I was an
ex-cop, and I was going to check him
out. If he liked the sample, which I
knew he would, he should let Patwell
know. Patwell would then let me know,
and we could proceed with the deal.

I made a major mistake with Vahjen. I
became friends with him. I should have
kept Harry strictly as a customer. Vahjen
was young, twenty-one, and had a lot
of learning to do about being discreet.
Vahjen introduced other dealers to me.
With so many customers I would sometimes
run dry early on a Friday night. This
forced me to find suppliers on Long Island
to fill the voids.

After the first deal was consummated, the plan was to
have Vahjen drive Ken home. The men took a detour and
stopped at a bar before getting to Ken's.

"One beer only," Ken said. "We've got coke in the trunk."

"Yeah. Sure, Kenny."

Ken finished his beer and couldn't find Vahjen, until he
stepped outside. There was the kid, sitting in the car partying
with three friends.

"Yo, get these fucking losers out of the car! How stupid
can you be? Just what I need is the cops to see you four
assholes. They would search the trunk and find coke!

"Take me home we're fucking through!"

Vahjen apologized. Ken wasn't having it. But a month
later they were back in business.

"In my head I knew it was time to quit, but instead I let
greed take over."

# CHAPTER 22. OPERATION LOSER

Physically and psychologically, Suffolk County is a long way from New York City, and at its gateway in West Babylon, a town of wide lots, green lawns, and safe streets. Suffolk County might as well be another planet. On any given morning a visitor could find moms pushing their strollers on the wide sidewalks of Little East Neck Road, past family-owned delis, bakeries, Italian restaurants, and salons or their husbands at work on their cars or shooting the shit over bagels and coffee.

This is cop land. Before 1962, New York City police officers were required to live in one of the five boroughs—Staten Island, Brooklyn, Queens, Manhattan, or the Bronx. The rules were relaxed allowing them to commute from the northern suburbs or Long Island, and the exodus began. Long Island suburbs like West Babylon may as well have had a Blue Wall built around them. These were suburbs where cops and their families were away from the shit of the city, and they preferred it that way.

It wasn't like the cops were any better in Suffolk County, it's just that the citizens were better behaved than their counterparts in the city. Suffolk County deputies didn't use their firearms much. They were more adept at firing off a radar gun and going after speeders on Montauk Highway than they were at bracing murder suspects or pulling felony stops on a car load of armed robbery suspects. When it came to the NYPD cops in their jurisdiction, county deputies were expected to smooth over domestic disputes, make sure drunks got home safe after a night at the bar, and never ask too many questions.

In summer the gas lamps on Little East Neck are adorned with flowers. Although close to the beach, it seems like every other house in West Babylon has a swimming pool. Ken's and Dori's home on Westchester Avenue was one of those. Shaded with trees, the two-story Hi-Ranch with its unique floor plan and roof was the couple's pride and joy.

Set back from the street, their home was adorned with wood siding on the top floor and built with solid brick on the ground. Visitors reached the single front door by climbing a set of concrete steps. Three windows on the top floor facing toward the front gave a 180-degree view of the street if anyone inside the house cared what was going on outside. NYPD cops had such little regard for their counterparts in Suffolk County that when surveillance was set up on Ken and his business partners, no one really noticed at first—and if they did, they didn't pay much attention.

It was now early 1992. And Suffolk County cops decided to stake out Ken's place after they got a tip about the operation from a snitch.

"I can put you in with this guy Harry Vahjen," the snitch told detectives. "He's just a kid, but he's moving a lot of product."

The next evening undercover cops made a buy from Vahjen at his home in East Islip, a few towns over from Babylon and quite a bit ritzier.

Suffolk County's narcotics bureau chief Robert Ewald hated dope. He had standing orders to his troops to keep cocaine (and the criminals that dealt it) out of Long Island. It didn't take rocket science to follow those orders. Young and arrogant, Vahjen was an easy mark. Not long after they turned their snitch, detectives set up a wire on the young man's telephone. Next, detectives had the snitch introduce Vahjen to an undercover cop who would make the case. He got lucky and met Ken too.

No deal was done during that first meeting, but Ken opened the door to exposing the whole operation. As he watched the undercover cop leave Vahjen's house, Ken wrote down his license number, then called his cousin, the Brooklyn cop in the Seven Three.

"I need you to run a plate for me," Kenny said. "I'll come over and get it tonight; we need to know who we are dealing with."

The detectives listening in on the wire were stunned.

"That's a cop talking. Holy Shit!"

"He just fucking called a New York City police precinct and asked them to run the plate of our undercover guy. What the fuck is going on here? Are the bad guys cops? Or are they on their own undercover operation?"

The detectives ran Kenny's plate. They got his name and address. They learned he was retired NYPD.

Suffolk County called NYPD. They wanted to make sure they weren't breaking in on a separate undercover operation that they didn't know about. They weren't. The Internal Affairs cops opened up a new investigation. This time their target was Kenny's cousin, the cop who ran the plate.

It took just a few hours for the cops to get a Suffolk County judge to issue a wiretap order on Ken's house.

As for Ken and Mike Dowd, they were still in touch with each other: hitting the bars, setting up deals, and doing what they could to maintain their cocaine income. They'd been watched for years by NYPD, but neither man had a clue that the deputies out on Long Island were now on their asses.

Suffolk County detectives were listening in when Dowd called. Four words into the first recording they had a title for their sting: Operation Loser.

"Hello loser," Dowd said.

"Hello loser," Ken replied.

When Dowd and Eurell were partners in an NYPD

patrol car, a lot of their work brought them into contact with organized crime, but these were mostly Latin American criminals that dealt drugs and handled their business in that world. Dowd explained that this time he had a problem that needed Italian muscle—maybe even mobster John Gotti's top guy. Dowd knew Ken could make the introduction.

Back when he was a kid working on construction sites, Kenny met Sammy "The Bull" Gravano. America would come to learn of Sammy as the brawn behind the ascent of John Gotti in the Gambino Crime Family. Kenny knew him as a relative, as Sammy was married to his cousin.

He once mentioned the connection to Dowd.

It's one of those things partners tend to discuss when they are sitting around in a patrol car waiting for something to happen. If he thought Dowd would forget it or not use it later, Kenny would have been sadly mistaken.

Kenny and Mike's relationship was symbiotic, and they relied on each other to help them pull off money making scams.

When Dowd wanted to get rid of the flashy red Corvette, he bragged about how he sold it to a chop shop. The deal earned Dowd $3,000 for the car and more when he filed an insurance claim alleging the Corvette had been stolen.

When Ken wanted to help out a buddy who needed to sell his Trans Am on the side, Dowd made the connection for Ken with the chop shop. That was small time. But Dowd came to Ken in need of a Gambino-sized favor.

One of his former partners had moved to Florida and had convinced Dowd to invest in a bagel shop there. Problems arose when a local cold cut distributor began to strong arm the little bagel shop.

"Dowd wanted to see if I would reach out to Sammy and get him to lean on the distributor."

That would have been one hell of a scary visit. Gravano,

a made man and John Gotti's capo, admitted whacking nineteen guys. The distributor would have known who he was. He probably would have shit his pants.

```
     Even  if  I  had  such  a  relationship
where  I  could  approach  Sammy  with  this
problem,  I  would  have  never  insulted  him
by  going  to  him  with  such  a  trivial
problem.  Plus  I  wasn't  about  to  put
myself  on  the  line  to  owe  a  favor  for
Dowd.  But  I  told  Dowd,  "Sure  I'll  see
what  I  can  do."
```

Ken hoped the problem in Florida would go away. Two weeks after the first call, Dowd was on the phone again.

"Kenny, can you do anything about this deal down in Florida?"

"Yeah. That's not happening."

"Thanks for trying. We'll go in a different direction."

Ken never heard about the situation again and gradually moved away from directly dealing coke, but was hooked on the income it provided. He continued to make the connections between suppliers like Dowd and dealers like Vahjen. But that was it.

"I'm not going to touch the stuff anymore," the Suffolk detectives heard Ken say in one of the wiretapped conversations. "Harry is going to do that now, and I'm going to charge him."

It was as if Ken had set up a franchise, and Vahjen was going to pay a fee for his connections, his advice, and protection.

```
     Business  was  moving  very  fast  for  me.
I  had  civilian  dealers  like  Vahjen  buying
cocaine  and  occasionally  crack  when  it  was
```

available. My other customers included electricians, plumbers, construction workers and school teachers. Cocaine had no boundaries.

Once I started moving in that Long Island drug circle it seemed everyone I met was not only doing coke but all of them were running a scam. A customer who worked for the power company showed me how to remove my electric meter and flip it upside down essentially running the meter numbers in reverse for free electricity. Another customer was a mailman who wanted to trade freshly stolen credit cards.

One of my regular dealers felt close to me eventually revealed his darkest secret. "I only told this to one other person," he said. "I killed someone." I don't know why he told me, and maybe it was because of the closeness you develop being in criminal activity together. Maybe it was fact that I let it be known to all my customers I was a former cop dealing drugs. Maybe he was just making it up hoping to get a reputation for being a badass. Whatever the reason was, I stopped him in his tracks. "Don't say another word; it's not something I want to know about." He hugged me and we did a shot.

On the other end of the spectrum I was still dealing with police officers like my cousin and his partner. They were doing raids just like I use to do with Dowd.

Any drugs or guns they stole in these raids they gave to me to move. I had a pretty good business. When suppliers in the city would run dry I bought coke from suppliers on Long Island. This would be a cause of concern for Dowd, who would complain that Long Island was weak. To me it didn't matter because it would sell. Anyway, I didn't personally use coke. Dowd, on the other hand, he used as much as he sold. He would want the purest form for that high. He was building quite a tolerance to it.

The scams were never-ending. My cousin had a friend who worked for a large insurance company. This woman would create bogus insurance files for fictitious clients. The files would show they were up to date for full coverage on an automobile. She would then put in a claim and issue a check for a total loss on the vehicle. She was unable to cash the checks because these fictitious clients lacked real ID.

I was close friends with the owner of a check cashing business in Manhattan. My cousin was aware of this and asked me to try and run the checks through the check cashing store. I wanted to be positive my contact wasn't going to be left high and dry by cashing checks that would later bounce. Once I was assured the checks were valid I made the deal. This is how it worked when the cancelled check would go back to the insurance company: The female who worked there would then shred the check along with the entire bogus file she created. No paper trail, the money just vanishes into thin air. Everyone in the chain got a cut. These checks were usually in amounts ranging from $5,000.00 to $15,000.00. I was amazed at how often we got away with this. White collar crime it seemed so much easier and cleaner.

Ken and his contacts kept on scamming oblivious to the fact that the Suffolk County detectives had evidence that Dowd, Eurell, Dowd's partner Mascia, and Ken's cousin were involved in the cocaine trade. They got a wire for Dowd's home telephone and began piecing together the relationships. Dowd bragged in the city that he was drug dealer in the country. When he was out in the boonies, he bragged about being a cop.

Since Vahjen was doing the heavy lifting, the cops' cocaine cartel began pooling their money to buy more and more coke. At one point the profits were so sweet they could have branched out into Atlantic City.

Ken began to sense that he and Dowd were about to be caught. How it started coming together, might have been a scene right out of *Goodfellas*—except it was going down in real life.

On a Sunday morning while going to my parents' home for breakfast, I spotted two plainclothes police detectives sitting up the block from my house. As I turned the corner, the unmarked car pulled away from the curb and drove up behind my new Lincoln. I quickly pulled to the side and forced the detectives to pass us. As they did I took down the plate number so I could run it and confirm who was watching me. I'm yelling at my wife, "Get a pen! Write this plate down."

We needed a way out.

Dowd, who now realized he was also being followed, discussed an investment plan with me and his partner. We would provide the money for a dealer in the city who would buy and sell cocaine. The investment and profit would then be returned to us.

This is exactly what I did with Harry Vahjen, only on a much larger scale. We pooled together enough money for five keys—almost $100,000.

Throughout the United States in the 1990s, most especially in its urban centers, relations between police departments and the mostly black and Latino residents of those neighborhoods from the Crown Heights in Brooklyn to South Central Los Angeles were at an all-time low.

On April 29, 1992, Los Angeles burst into flames. A jury in Simi Valley acquitted four LAPD officers accused of beating motorist Rodney King after a high-speed chase that ended in Lakeview Terrace. The beating, caught on videotape, sparked a national debate over use of force by Los Angeles Police officers and brought federal scrutiny to the department because of its institutional racism.

The scrutiny also exposed drug corruption in the LAPD's Rampart Division that wasn't unlike the sort of corruption going down in Brooklyn.

But as LA burned that night, videotape was about to bring down more officers. Dowd was caught on camera in uniform making the buy. Later he was heard to say as he listened to news reports about the unrest in Los Angeles, "If I had caught Rodney King, that bastard never would have gotten up."

# CHAPTER 23. THE HOUSE THAT COKE BUILT

On May 6, 1992, newspapers around the country carried similar stories about the "Loser's Club" a group of NYPD officers arrested by the lowly Suffolk County Sheriff's Department on suspicion of operating a multimillion-dollar drug ring.

Suffolk County did the thing NYPD could never do, they arrested Mike Dowd when he was high on cocaine and drunk. They found a bindle of coke in his uniform and a package in his locker. At Dowd's home, investigators took $20,000 cash and a 9 mm pistol with the serial number filed off.

Mikey D kept the phone numbers for Adam Diaz and Baron Perez in his bureau.

Kenny was arrested at Vahjen's pad on Garretson in East Islip. Suffolk County took his Lincoln, his Corvette, and his wife's Chevy. They also took his freedom.

Ken's cousin was taken into custody at work as was Dowd's partner.

Although she knew little about the scope or size of what was going on with Ken and Mike, Dori was arrested at home in connection with the caper.

They were all taken and booked at Suffolk County's Dennison building, a location the deputies typically used to hold drunks.

Dori had one thing to say when she saw Ken: "I told you this would happen."

Dowd demanded respect.

"How about a little professional courtesy here?" One of the officers yelled at the detectives. "We're all cops here."

A lieutenant shot back.

"You are an embarrassment. You don't belong on the police department; you belong in jail."

The next morning, Suffolk County held a press conference.

"These guys were drug dealers who happened to have police uniforms," prosecutor Robert F. Ewald said "This is not a case of someone who once said 'I know where I can get you some coke.' These were dealers in the business of getting coke."

```
     It's  amazing  how  much  you  learn
after  you  are  arrested.  I  had  a  female
acquaintance  tell  me  how  she  did  coke
with  one  of  the  Suffolk  county  prosecutors
when  they  were  back  in  college.  It  didn't
matter.  He  wasn't  dealing  and  didn't  get
caught.  We  were  and  now  we  were  about  to
pay  the  price.
```

NYPD meanwhile scrambled to do the damage control it hoped to avoid. The spin the commissioner's office put on it was, "Hey, this happened in Long Island; these guys were crafty enough to outsmart us."

When IAD Chief Robert Beatty was asked directly about Dowd, he said the unit never had enough information to roll him

"We did look at him, but we couldn't tag him," Beatty told reporters. "Sometimes you have to marshal all of your forces finally to succeed. With guys like Michael Dowd, something like this is what it takes. It's important to note that these individuals were acting on their own."

Before Dori was released on her own recognizance—and not charged—Ken reassured her.

"Everything will be OK."

His first court appearance gave Ken an idea of how deep the case went.

> In court I saw my mother and father, my aunt and uncle, and Dowd's wife, Bonnie. I gave a quick nod to my parents to let them know I was OK. Bail was set at $350,000 for me and Dowd, $250,000 for Mascia, and $150,000 for everyone else.

Ken and Dowd were put in protective custody. They learned that fifty people had been arrested in Operation Loser, many were casual drug users who were caught on tape placing orders with Vahjen. The rest were cops.

Almost as soon as they hit the lockup, Ken ran into Walter Yurkiw, the former cop who worked the Seven Five with Dowd but was convicted for his role in the robbery of a bodega and the kidnapping of the Bodega's owner.

"How did you get caught up in this?" Ken asked.

"I didn't" Big Walter replied. "I'm in here on another beef."

Walter was accused in the March robbery of a Long Island man. The newspapers were reporting that no one really gave a shit about the chicken shit drug burn. The cops wanted Walter to rat out his former brothers. He wouldn't and wound up back in state prison.

It took a while for Ken to make bail, and there were several false starts. One weekend, Kenny and Mike got released with the hopes of getting a reduced bail amount that would allow them to stay home until there was some court action. Ken was ecstatic and relieved.

> As I entered the house my daughter

was at the top of the stairs. When she saw me she broke into a hysterical cry, a happy hysterical cry. She was stomping her little feet up and down while reaching out with her arms. It was a very long time in the life of an 18-month-old not to see the person who took care of her every day. I picked her up in my arms, hugged her tightly, and walked off to another room to have a good cry with her. It absolutely broke my heart. What have I done? I assured my little girl: "Everything is OK; Daddy's staying home."

On Monday afternoon, Ken was back in jail. His bail wasn't reduced. Neither was Dowd's.

Ken needed to come up with $300,000. Dowd needed to put together $325,000.

I turned to my wife and handed her my wallet, St. Christopher's medal, keys to the borrowed car. Then I whispered to her, "I love you, do you know the way home?"

Reporters surrounded Dori as she left the courthouse. They wanted to know what I said.

"I drove away as fast as I could," said Dori. "Once I was away from all those people, I pulled over to the side of the road, and I just sat there and cried. I didn't think I would ever stop crying."

Reporters began doing what reporters do best, they dug through the case and generated stories. The *New York Post* ran lurid accounts of Dowd's and Eurell's exploits. Most were written by Mike McAlary, who would later turn his series of columns on the case into the book *Good Cop, Bad Cop*.

In one of his pieces, headlined "The House that Coke Built," which was penned while Ken and Mikey D were still in the Suffolk County Jail, McAlary described a meeting he had with Dowd's former girlfriend, who had been a cop in the Seven Five. The two met in a coffee shop back in 1989, long before anyone outside the NYPD had ever heard of Mike Dowd or Ken Eurell.

Dowd's former lover told McAlary how they flew to the Dominican to set up a coke deal. She explained to McAlary that there was an infestation of coke dealers in the department—led by Dowd. She wanted the reporter to know that she wanted out of the bad shit that was going on, but she wasn't going to commit suicide like O'Regan did when the Seven Seven came crashing down.

McAlary wrote that he didn't necessarily believe her. The *New York Post* reporter then went on to detail how a pair of his colleagues interviewed Walter Yurkiw after the botched bodega robbery and kidnapping of Braulio Lugo, the store owner. The reporters said Yurkiw, who appeared to be high, told of drug dealing, contract murders, and patrol car orgies with hookers. McAlary wrote that he wished he had followed up back then.

The piece led with a painstaking and breathless, if envious, description of Dowd's neighborhood and his house at 28 Norton Avenue in Port Jefferson. Dowd's castle was a yellow, two-story colonial on an acre of prime real estate at the end of a cul-de-sac in an exclusive neighborhood. The house that coke built was impressive indeed.

Under the subhead "How Cocaine Cops Got to Easy Street," McAlary began: "The towering yellow colonel sits on a knoll at the end of a cul-de-sac. When a car passes the adjoining houses at the end of Norton Avenue in Port Jefferson a set of motion detectors ignite a domino string of harsh spotlights. Crime cannot survive on this block.

"The paint on the renovated house is new and almost wet to the touch. The place has the clean, crisp smell of money. The grass on the one-acre lot is as neatly manicured as a police cadet's hair."[7]

McAlary's next piece, "Dirtiest Cop Ever," also appeared on the *Post's* front page. The headline, done in 100-plus point type—all caps—was accompanied by a double-chinned black and white mugshot of Dowd that made him seem every bit the sleaze that the headline alleged. The column said Dowd helped an unidentified drug kingpin set up the execution of a Bronx coke dealer who didn't pay his bills. McAlary described Dowd as "the most corrupt cop in the history of the NYPD."

Apparently the reporter never heard of 1912's Charles Becker.

The story infuriated Kenny, who confronted Dowd over its contents. Dowd had other stuff on his mind and told Kenny they needed to take care of Vahjen, who was in the jail's general population.

"I think that will be useless," Kenny said.

"Then let's burn down his parent's fucking house," Dowd said. "That'll teach the little prick a lesson."

The stories in the newspaper continued to mount. Then David Letterman made mention of the case. On his highly rated *Late Show with David Letterman*, the comedian took on Dowd and Eurell in his monologue.

"The New York Police Department has a new recruitment slogan: 'Become a policeman and earn up to $8,000 a week

7    McAlary, Mike "The House that Coke Built", New York Post, Wednesday May 13, 1992

in your spare time.'"

Dowd continued to pace his cell. He was focused on taking care of business and explained to Kenny that there was a drug dealer in the 94th Precinct that needed to be dealt with. Money was involved, but who owed who was unclear. Dowd suggested a preemptive strike. He didn't want the dealer cooperating with the Suffolk County detectives who had an already airtight case.

"We gotta break his wife's legs," Dowd said. "Then this fuck will shut the fuck up."

Dowd's friends had seen their coke-addled friend act weird before, but this behavior was something new. Maybe he was going through withdrawals.

"He's fucking lost it" Ken told Mascia. "He must be scared shitless."

The detectives had uniformed Officers Dowd and Mascia on videotape buying drugs. They had audio of Ken making deals on the phone. They had Vahjen and all of the losers he and the others guys were selling to on Long Island. As far as the cops were concerned, Dowd and Eurell were the kingpins, which is why their bails were the highest.

Dowd had a pretty good idea of what was in store for him if a conviction came down—twenty-five years to life. Ken figured that for his role in the scam he'd do a maximum of eight, but he planned on working out a plea deal.

Dowd bailed out first. Ken followed. Dori paid the bondsman. They put up their house on Long Island and Ken's parents' house as collateral. A mutual fund left to Dori and Ken as part of her father's estate also helped pay the bond.

Dori handled all the paperwork.

I didn't want to use our money for bail. I told Dori, 'Just let me sit here.' I was prepared to do the time,

and in jail I was already getting time
off my sentence.

Dori wouldn't have it. She bailed Ken out and brought
him home.
It was a smart move.

That saved me. Dori hired me an
excellent lawyer, spared no expense, and
I was intelligent enough to take all his
experience and advice. Primarily he told
me to stay the fuck away from Dowd.

## CHAPTER 24. THE CONFESSIONAL

Ken's attorneys told him to stay the fuck away from Dowd. No one told Dowd to stay away from Ken.

> Mike and I decided to go out to dinner one last time. This time though there would be no expensive restaurant with $4,000 or $5,000 in our pockets. There was just enough money for dinner and a few drinks with the wives.

Dowd was loving his freedom and insisting there was no way in hell that he was going back to jail

"I got a deal for us, Ken," said Dowd "All we gotta do is hit the stash house of this dope dealer. I know the guy."

Dowd elaborated the plan which, at its climax, had Ken and Mike kidnapping the wife of a deadbeat dope dealer, turning her over to the Columbians, then taking their own families and escaping to Nicaragua. Taken at face value, it sounded far-fetched and absurd.

"You're fucking crazy," Ken said.

"No. Kenny I'm serious," Dowd said, his voice rapidly rising to a manic pitch, "We've got jobs lined up with this buddy of mine who is shrimping and exports seafood back to the states. It's perfect. We'll make $1,000 a week. We'll be fucking kings down there."

Yeah, right. Well, it's possible Dowd knows what he's saying, possible that this isn't wishful thinking born of desperation and sleep deprivation. But even if true, if Ken were to accept the offer and vanish to Central America, his folks would lose their home.

"Shit Kenny, my family would rather lose their houses than see me go to jail for twenty-five years," Dowd said. "I bet your family feels the same way."

Ken imagined himself sitting down with Mom and Dad and saying "I can escape from America, run away to a shrimp boat, be free, but you lose your home and I never see you again."

Crap.

"We should just plead out, Mike. Do our time. We earned it."

"There is no fucking way," Dowd was screaming now, and everyone's skin felt too tight.

"You think I'm going away for twenty-five fucking years. No fucking way!"

It wasn't just the Suffolk case that hung over their heads. All their criminal deeds in the Seven Five were coming home to roost.

The US Attorney's Office had a file open since at least 1991. They knew that Dowd once schemed to earn $10,000 by getting me to drive a shipment of cocaine across the country Smokey and the Bandit style. I turned it down.

A bigger and more pressing concern was that the Feds had guys from Diaz's organization already in prison who were willing to sing like the Vienna Boys' Choir if it would shave some time off their sentences.

Diaz didn't tell the cops anything they didn't already know.

"I caught close to ten years long before all this shit happened with Mike and Kenny's case. I was willing to take a plea, but one of my men, Victor, refused," Diaz explained. "He told me that if the government was willing to enter into a plea deal with me it meant they didn't have shit for a case. Victor fought it. They gave him twenty years for being guilty of attempted murder."

That move really hurt Adam Diaz. When he went to court with his plea deal in place, the judge wouldn't accept it. "He said he'd already heard so much about me that he wouldn't agree to the deal. I answered questions, but I didn't cooperate with the FBI," Diaz said. "When Mike and Ken got arrested, I knew better than to fuck with these people."

The fact that Ken and Mike were being looked at by the Feds didn't surprise Adam one bit.

"I knew it was going to happen."

The feds saw blood in the water. They knew that uniformed NYPD officers selling cocaine on Long Island was a conspiracy and likely met all the requirements of a RICO case that they typically brought against Mafiosos like John Gotti and Sammy "The Bull."

In early July, Ken sat down with prosecutors in the US Attorney's Office for the Southern District of New York. There were conditions if he wanted to reduce his sentence. In his dealings with the feds, Ken had to tell them the truth, and he had to tell them every bad thing he had ever done.

Ken called Dowd to give him a heads up.

"What the hell do they want?" Dowd wanted to know.

"My lawyer thought it would be a good idea to sit down and see what they have."

"Fuck that, Kenny."

"We can't ignore it, Mike."

Hours later Ken was meeting with investigators.

"From the questions they asked me it was obvious they had already spoken with someone else. I figured it was Diaz and his people," Ken said. "I was correct."

Mascia, who had been Dowd's partner at the end, was also talking. The process of cooperating became a chess game of sorts, and Kenny was thinking several moves ahead.

"If Mascia were to cooperate, that would be evidence against Dowd, which could lead to Dowd turning against me. It was just a matter of time as to who the Feds would get to first."

Ken went home from that first meeting with a lot on his mind.

Dowd and his wife, Bonnie, were practically standing on Ken and Dori's front doorstep when Ken got back to Long Island.

"What happened with the Feds?" Dowd demanded. His wife, Bonnie, handed Dori a letter.

Ken didn't hold anything back.

"I had a meeting. They wanted to know everything we did as partners in the Seven Five."

"What the fuck did you tell them?"

"Not much. We walked out after ten minutes," Ken explained.

"Fuck, Kenny, that's all the more reason we should do this thing and then go to Nicaragua," Mike replied and told Ken that if he agreed to go, Bonnie would feel better about the move.

Dori sensed that Bonnie wasn't too keen on leaving the country. She read the letter as Bonnie stared out the bay window in the upstairs living room.

"It was a good-bye letter really," Dori said. "I may have looked calm while reading it, but inside I was seething. Mike's behavior was outrageous beyond belief. I mean he was far away in his craziness, beyond the beyond and then some."

Dori paused in the midst of her recollections to assess Dowd's craziness.

"If he just stopped for a moment and saw the looks in all of our eyes, he would have known it was never going to happen—no one is running off to Nicaragua to peel shrimp. I couldn't keep my mouth shut—I've never excelled at that—I confronted Mike about his attitude and Bonnie's reluctance to leave everything behind."

"Yeah, she ain't too excited about it," Mike admitted. "In the beginning she wanted to go, I told her 'You're not the one doing the fucking time. I am!'"

While Dori and Mike discussed Bonnie as if she weren't sitting right in front of them, Ken picked up the torn piece of yellow legal pad paper on which Bonnie wrote her letter. He read a few lines. Just one stood out:

"The four of us have become such great friends," Bonnie wrote. "Who knows if we'll be able to remain friends through all of this?"

Had Ken been Robbie the Robot from *Lost in Space*, Dori and Mike's conversation would have been interrupted by cries of "Danger Will Robinson! Danger!" Ken, reading between the lines, decoded the question as an involuntary warning of "You are about to get fucked." Suddenly, Ken's imagination was on fire creating catastrophic worst-case scenarios

*Mike is cooperating with the Feds! This drug stickup and bail skip is a setup. No one in their right mind robs a drug dealer, kidnaps his wife, turns her over to be murdered, and skips bail to Nica-fucking-ragua!*

The plan was insane. He and Dori already discussed it. Mike was serious, or seriously lying to himself. This wasn't how it was supposed to go, this wasn't anything he or Mike or their wives saw coming. But to turn on Mike was another issue. The thought of ratting this insane plot of his out to the Feds was a nightmare.

Dori advised Ken of one timeless truth: All laws and

loyalties may be sacrificed to save someone's life. That, in truth, was the bottom line, the final straw, the last overworked metaphor. You draw the ethical line somewhere, and the line keeps moving with each self-serving rationalization. For Ken Eurell, this was the end of the line. He would cooperate. If Dowd went through with this plan, not only would the deceased dealer's wife be murdered, most likely so would Mike. The Columbians were not known for letting witnesses live. Giving up the kidnapping scheme to the Feds was a sickening thought; Mike being killed by the Columbians along with this nameless widow was worse.

Ken called his lawyer. Then he went to the same church where Dori, Mike, Bonnie, and Ken celebrated his daughter's baptism.

"Father, I have some real sins to confess ..." This wasn't the made up confession of a six-year-old, this was reality spoken aloud and acknowledged. Ken recited his litany of wrongdoing, his career as a cop, his friendship with Mike Dowd, their partnership with Perez and Diaz, the robberies, the lies, deception, betrayals, and the lucrative dealing of illegal drugs.

"Speak the truth. Deceive no more. Start a clean slate on life," the priest advised. "With so many people involved, it will eventually be out in the open. You shouldn't feel guilty about your friend. You are both in the positions you are in because of who you are."

True. I couldn't blame Mike for anything.

Dowd didn't make us become partners, he didn't make me take payoffs. Everything I did was my choice, my decision. I

did it myself. I can't blame him for
anything.

The next morning Ken laid it out for prosecutors David
Fein and Robert Rice. They told him to be completely
truthful. He was.

I told them all about my career from
start to finish. It was typical Joe Cop
until the Michael Dowd years. When I
started explaining how we received $8,000
a week in drug payoffs, everyone's ears
perked up. Clearly they didn't expect
to hear such established and detailed
corruption from a beat cop.

They wondered how Dowd was able to get through a piss
test if he was high on the job all the time. Kenny explained
that his partner, whom he described as a sort of evil genius,
had rigged up a "whizinator" with a mustard bottle. The
device allowed Mike to store clean piss and use it to his
advantage.

As the story wound to its conclusion, Ken laid out Dowd's
current plan to knock over a stash house, deliver a woman
for execution, and flee to Nicaragua where they would be
reborn as Forrest Gump-esque shrimp boat captains making
$1,000 a week in the "export" business.

The attorneys and investigators in the room listened
with rapt attention. They were shocked that Dowd wanted to
commit more crimes while he was out on bail.

"Fucking arch criminal," one investigator exclaimed as
Kenny described the plot.

In "crime think," being out on bail is the best time to
commit crime because it is not expected, especially by

someone in law enforcement, and makes even more sense if that crime frees you from prosecution, frees you from potential prison time, and relocates you and your loved ones to a pleasant country with no extradition treaty with the USA. Were it not for the superficial absurdity of the plan, and the willingness to have a woman sacrificed over her dead husband's drug debt, the plan made perfect sense.

US Attorney David Fein and DEA Agent Mike Troster decided to go to Suffolk County and convince the deputies to turn their case against Dowd and Eurell into a racketeering indictment similar to those used against the mafia and criminal street gangs.

"Ken, you are going to have to keep us in the loop from here on in," the prosecutor explained. "We'll need you to come back here in a few days and pick up a micro recorder from the DEA."

Ken was going to wear a wire. He was going to tape everything Dowd said, and they were going to use it against Dowd, who had clearly become a brazen and out-of-control criminal—or at least that's what Ken had to believe to do the most unthinkable of all acts—tear down the Blue Wall and turn on his partner.

Ken didn't think the meeting would end quite the way it did.

```
    It was one thing to tell them all I
knew, in fact it felt good to talk about
it, get it in the open, and get it off my
chest. It was another to wear a wire and
put myself in danger.
```

It was strange to be wired up to meet with his best friend and longtime partner in crime.

> In the beginning of our partnership.
> I suspected Dowd was wearing a wire to
> catch me.

Ken, wearing a wire to catch Mike, knew the ridicule he would face from his buddies still in the New York Police Department. He also knew the dangers of wearing a wire on the street—those were significant.

It did cross Ken's mind that he and Mike were so similar that Dowd may already suspect him of wearing a wire—a suspicion easily confirmed.

> I knew if I was caught wearing a wire
> they would have no problem killing me
> and the DEA wasn't going to be around to
> see it.

# CHAPTER 25. DANNY, HECTOR, AND RAY

The NYPD and the DEA set up surveillance. The cops and agents were determined to prevent Dowd from ripping off a stash house in Queens, kidnapping a woman, and/or fleeing the country.

"Perhaps other corrupt cops or corrupt DEA agents saw that stash house as a well-deserved perk," joked former New Jersey Police Officer Fred Wolfson, "I'm kidding, of course. I'm sure law enforcement corruption doesn't exist at the Federal level."

One of the first things learned was that Dowd was renting out rooms in his house. There is no law against renting out rooms in your home, but the names of his renters were of interest. Agents identified Dowd tenants as "Danny," "Hector," and "Ray." They learned that Danny had an interest in the Queens stash house; Hector had an active drug case in Louisiana; Ray was Pablo Escobar's main guy in New York. These were heavy hitters, and they meant business.

Dowd had a more sinister motive than robbery. There would be a kidnapping as well—a kidnapping ending in torture and murder.

Mike wanted Kenny to meet the team and go over the plan. The eventual meeting took place on Monday, July 27, 1992.

Almost as soon as the introductions were over, Dowd went into detail about the job. Johnny, who once lived at the target house in Queens, disappeared with ten kilos of coke that had been fronted to him by Ray on behalf of the Colombians. Ray was on the hook for the scam, and the Colombians explained that if he didn't pay with his life, somebody would have to be sacrificed. That someone was Johnny's wife.

That's how it worked. This wasn't an eye for an eye shit. This was "fuckers are going to be taught a lesson." It's guaranteed that lesson would have involved any one of the gruesome and notorious tortures the Colombians employed with dramatic effect.

Ray had been tailing the woman for several weeks. He knew her routine. He knew when she was home. How long she stayed there, where she went when she was gone, and who visited her when she was home.

They agreed on a plan. Danny, Hector, and Ray would pose as flower delivery men and enter the woman's house. Dowd and Eurell would stay outside with a scanner monitoring police activity—if any.

Danny, Hector, and Ray would grab any cash, guns, or drugs they could get, then grab the woman.

"She'll be executed, and my debt will be paid," Ray explained.

In exchange for their help as the outside men, Dowd and Ken would get an equal share of any drugs or cash that the men grabbed while they were inside.

When they got back to Long Island, Kenny pulled Dowd aside for a reality check. The conversation was caught on tape.

"Mike, what the fuck?" Ken asked. "The Colombians might fucking do everybody. They don't want no witnesses after they do this broad."

"Fuck them," Mike responded. "I'll fucking kill them if they fucking move wrong, they got money too, Kenny. You've got to realize not many people can kill somebody. You understand?"

"Not really Mike. I don't understand why you want to be there when the broad is fucking turned over," Ken replied.

"I didn't really. These fucking Colombians would love to have us. What are you kidding me?"

"Can you trust these fucking guys?" Ken asked.

Dowd explained that he was brought in by Hector's sister Marge, who "called me up when she found out I was in fucking trouble."

"Margie spoke to me and said, 'Mike, look, I know you're in trouble for what you've been fucking doing, my brothers are involved in that, if you want to do something with them, they can help you, you can help them."

Ken listened to what Mike was saying, and he knew he wasn't getting through. He knew the Colombians didn't give a shit about either of them. Mike just didn't get it.

Then, something happened that neither Mike nor Ken planned for—some other crew used Mike's ambush idea. It was all over the news: A Queens woman was slain by a gunman who posed as a flower deliveryman. That was exactly Mike's plan. As soon as he heard of the shooting, Dowd called Kenny. Again, the conversation was caught on tape.

"I'm pissed off, Kenny," Mike announced.

"How come?"

"The motherfucker beat us to the punch, that's what pissed me off."

Now, anybody posing as a flower deliveryman would be suspicious. Even so, the partners had work to do and settled on doing a dry run.

It went without a hitch. On the way back to Long Island, Dowd insisted on stopping in the Seven Five for a drink. Kenny grabbed a Heineken. The owner of the bodega knew Ken and Mike from their cop days. Now they were famous. Just about every day one of them was pictured on the front page of the *Post*, the *Daily News,* or *Newsday.*

"Ayyyyyyyyyye Kenny!" Mamma Gracie called out

when they stepped in. She pointed to a religious shrine she set up on a shelf in the bodega. She explained the candles were lit for his benefit.

"Where's my fucking candle?" Dowd demanded.

Out front the five men discussed the plan one last time. They decided the kidnapping would go down on Thursday, July 30, just a few hours away.

Ken called his contact at the DEA, and he was told to meet with NYPD homicide detective Joe Hall in nearby Massapequa. Hall had worked in the Seven Five with Ken.

"I was embarrassed I had to meet somebody I had worked with," admitted Ken. Hall assured him that anyone in his position would do the exact same thing.

Ken felt somewhat better but went home edgy. If one little thing went wrong, he could be dead. Messing with the Colombians put his family in danger, too. He might have been wearing a wire, but he would be walking a tightrope.

The DEA assured Kenny that they would be close by. They would be on his side when the shit was going down. But what if? What if the wire failed? What if the DEA got waylaid? What if Dowd was being set up? What if Dowd was setting him up? This was not a great situation. In fact it sucked.

Dowd and Ken had been friends and partners. They had the sort of bond that is shared by men who have gone through combat together. Outside of work the duo had a lot in common. They were married about the same time. Their sons were the same age. They were business partners. They had seen a lot of shit get done, and they had seen even more shit go down.

Ken knew the Blue Wall protected him and his buddy when they were on the streets. But Dowd had now gone too far. He had to be stopped.

Ken tossed and turned in his bed. In his mind he was

going over the plan. He looked at it from every angle and prepared for anything that could go wrong. Just before dawn he was ready.

Dori got up early. She knew Ken was nervous. She was scared. They talked as Dori got an ACE bandage and strapped a DEA-supplied tape recorder to Ken's leg. It was snug, just below his calf.

```
    It fit in nicely because I have a
muscular calf. I then ran the wire up
my leg to my waist. I didn't run it
to my chest because I thought it might
be detected when Dowd and I hugged and
kissed hello.
```

Ken smiled for the first time in months.

"What could you possibly be smiling about?" Dori demanded.

"I feel like a cop again."

Ken dressed. Dori kissed him for good luck when Dowd arrived.

The two men set off for Queens. Tape was rolling, and it captured their conversation.

"What did you tell Bonnie?" Ken asked.

"Well, 'I'm going off to work,' that's what I told my wife. She goes, uh, 'I had plans today to do things.' I told her, 'I'm going to work.' And, she goes, 'Robbing somebody is not going to work.' And I said, 'Well it is this time.'"

Bonnie had hoped to get out of the house in time for an exercise class. She wanted Mike to watch the kids.

"I said, 'You exercise at home.' What pisses me off is, I said, 'If I had a regular job to go to today, you couldn't do this, you'd have to get a babysitter.'

"'But you don't have a regular job.'

"I said, 'Yes I do, this is my regular job now.'

"What I was going to say to her. I have to be rational—explain, you know what I mean. Like she was planning on daddy being home, well I ain't. 'Now go do something. I'll be home for your four o'clock fucking job. Other than that I got the whole day to myself.'"

Dowd said his mind raced all night. He didn't sleep well. He had shit to think about.

He was irritated that the Colombians didn't want to listen to his directions on the kidnapping.

"I laid down. I didn't go to sleep right away, but about twenty minutes after I laid down, I talked it over like three times. I said, 'That's enough. I'm just like them now. I'm going there blind; I don't give a fuck. They're the ones going in, I don't care. I'll leave. See ya.'"

Dowd continued to maneuver his car through traffic as they left Long Island and entered Queens. Ken turned on the scanner. Dowd continued his rant. He was pissed that they didn't want to listen but was counting on a score that would free him up to get a new start as a shrimp boat captain in Central America. Dowd was practically licking his chops at the end of his rant.

"I plan, but they don't listen to the plan," Dowd said. "They can go on their own. I'll still get money if they get in. The real worry is getting in the fucking door. After that, fuck everything. Once you're in her door man, it will be like a fucking picnic."

Two blocks away from the target's home. Ken perked up.

"Did you see that car circle around?" he asked.

"You think they're still following us?" Dowd was getting nervous.

"I don't see him now. Damn! Keep an eye in the mirror," Ken shot back.

It was a game. He wanted to make Dowd believe nothing

was different. Ken was usually suspicious. If he stopped being suspicious, that would be a problem.

Hours before Ken and Mike cruised into the neighborhood, DEA agents swept into the woman's house. They took her and several members of her family into protective custody. The agents then sat and waited like a spider for a fly.

For bad guys, a police scanner is a lifeline. It lets them know what's happening when they are casing a victim's home or business or when they are actively engaged in criminal activity. By the same token, a scanner can be an undercover cop's worst enemy—especially at the moment of truth. More than one undercover assignment has been blown by misguided talk on the police scanner.

As they neared the woman's house, Dowd's scanner crackled to life. Dispatch reported a suspicious car on Avon Street and assigned a patrol car to investigate.

Another voice spoke up.

"Disregard that 911 call. DEA has a surveillance underway on Avon Street."

Ken heard it and thought, "Shit. The cover just got compromised."

Dowd had a confused look on his face. He got nervous. The Colombians weren't around. That wasn't part of the plan.

"Do you think they set us up?" he asked.

Dowd immediately drove off. He found a payphone and placed a call to Bonnie. She told him she had a message from Hector, Ray, and Danny: They overslept.

Dowd, convinced the Colombians were setting him up, came back to the car cursing.

"Who fucking oversleeps when we're ready to go?"

Dowd was pumped with adrenalin. He jetted back out toward Long Island. Back on Avon Street the DEA was in a panic. Without a live wire to know exactly what went down, the agents wondered what the fuck just happened. Now they'd lost their inside man.

Worried that Ken's cover was exposed and he was in danger, they called Dori. She was scared.

"What do you mean you've lost him?" she wailed into the telephone.

A few minutes later, Dowd and Kenny arrived back at the Eurell home. It wasn't supposed to happen like this. Dori had the bags packed and sitting by the front door. She was relieved to see Ken, but Dowd was still dangerous. She did not want him to see the bags. It took five minutes to move them, then she put her hair under the faucet to make it appear as if she came out of the shower before opening the door.

"Good thing we had that fucking scanner," Dowd said as he walked in.

Then, holding his thumb and forefinger close enough to each other so that they nearly touched, Dowd added. "We came this close. They almost had us, Dor."

Agitated and restless, Dowd took off, saying he'd catch Ken later. What he meant exactly was not clear—did he mean catch up with Ken, or catch Ken in a lie?

Ken called the DEA and told them exactly how they blew their own cover, then took off for his lawyer's office. Dowd, suspicious, was catching up all right—he was catching up with Ken at the lawyer's office. Arriving hot on Ken's heals, Dowd barged in demanding answers.

The young office assistant almost wet himself.

"Dowd's here! Dowd's here! What should I do?"

"Let him in," Ken advised.

Dowd, agitated and angered, demanded an answer to one simple question.

"Are you fucking me?"

Ken had no time to answer. A staff member buzzed him on the office intercom.

"Mr. Eurell, pick up line two," the voice suggested.

On the line was attorney Eric Naiburg, the lawyer who was then representing Long Island Lolita Amy Fisher. A teenager, Fisher was dating an auto mechanic Joey Buttafucco and decided the only way she could be with Joey forever was to kill his wife, Mary Jo. She nearly pulled it off.

"Are you in any danger," Naiburg asked Ken.

Dowd was seething. To keep him calm, Ken pretended he was talking to Dori.

"No babe, everything is OK. I'm just waiting for my attorney to return from court."

Dowd, comforted by Ken's calm demeanor, began to deescalate his mood, reassuring himself that Kenny had his back covered, not stabbed. If there is one man he could trust, it was Ken Eurell.

In a masculine way of apologizing for his paranoid suspicion that Ken would fuck him, Mike Dowd gave Kenny a hug and smiled as if to say, "I know we're cool. We will be okay."

Watching Michael Dowd walk out the door, Ken Eurell knew what awaited his best friend, and he didn't have to be there to see it clearly in his mind's eye—the NYPD and DEA agents patiently waiting for Dowd to come home, then the siren-free parade of agent's vehicles arriving in his driveway. It would be uneventful, inglorious, and heartbreaking. There would be no getaway, no eluding armed guards at every frontier, no daring escape from the hand-cuff clutches of the law, no professional courtesy to let Dowd go on his way to a new life in Nicaragua.

"My partner got me, right?" Dowd wasn't asking, he was lamenting and confirming the worst possible scenario— betrayed by the one man he trusted, the one guy who would have his back. In his manic anger and hyper driven despair, Dowd was more hurt than angered. Not that he didn't suspect that Ken would turn on him. Hell, he suspected everyone would turn on him. So did Ken Eurell.

How many times did Ken think Mike was setting him up, how often did he and Dori consider the entire escape to Central America plan as an elaborate ruse? The difference between prudent caution and paranoia is simply that caution is prudent. Caution allows one to avoid danger by seeing situations clearly. The hyper vigilance associated with cocaine, the precursor to paranoia, is debilitating and confusing.

When you believe that no one can be trusted, you become untrustworthy,

# EPILOGUE

Kenny couldn't deal with Mike's arrest. It actually made him physically ill, and he was emotionally drained for days.

"Kenny had a hard time, obviously," Dori remembered. "He was heartbroken. They were really tight. But Michael was unstoppable. Something had to happen. Ken had a lot of lonely moments after that."

The Feds gave Kenny some options.

"What is important for me is to make people understand," Ken Eurell explained, "is that I didn't get arrested and then flip on Dowd. We were arrested together; I wasn't cooperating. And then, while out on bail, he came to me with this crazy Butch Cassidy and Sundance plan to kidnap a woman for execution, and then we would skip bail and live the good life in Nicaragua. That's when I decided to cooperate. I was in an impossible no-win situation once I became aware of a murder plot. For some reason that doesn't come across clear in the documentary, and some people think I was arrested then gave Dowd up. Not true, not true at all.

"After Dowd's arrest, Dori, I, and the kids were offered the witness protection program. I declined the government's offer. I didn't want to have my kids change their names and take their grandparents away from them. I moved my family out of state and remained in contact with the US Attorney for the next four years."

Although Dowd offered to cooperate with the federal investigation into NYPD corruption, the Feds found him to be "untruthful and evasive about his criminal conduct."

They began with an interview where Dowd exhibited some of the narcissism that characterized his personality.

What was additionally problematic was that his statements were 100 percent true.

"Other officers tried to cling to me," Dowd explained. "They chaperoned themselves around me. They wanted to know what I was doing. They wanted to be part of it."

Who wanted to be part of it? An investigator asked.

"Whoever knew me," Dowd answered.

A harsh federal court sentencing memorandum put together after that interview included some insight from Bonnie Dowd into her husband's personality.

"Michael is usually drinking twenty-three hours a day and throwing up during the other hour," Bonnie said, adding that Michael was involved in several extramarital affairs and was a heavy cocaine user.

"Dowd was on the run, drinking constantly, using cocaine, running around with his brother, and treating her badly," a portion of the government's memo read. "She described Dowd as a 'psycho' who has an infantile personality, and who never received the correct love and attention from his family. She feels that her husband's behavior is explained by his upbringing in that his parents did not give him love or friendship and always expected more from him."

Investigators learned that Dowd had a drinking problem that began when he was twelve years old.

"He stated at the age of twelve his friends had to carry him home because he was so drunk. He continued to drink on the weekends, and 'whenever he wanted to' he drank alcohol before he left for high school. ... He stated that he gets into trouble when he drinks alcohol."

Dowd also had a drug problem, investigators said.

"Dowd tried marijuana for the first time in the eighth grade. He smoked marijuana approximately three times a week for two years before he stopped using it. Approximately one year later he began to smoke marijuana again while in high school. He stated he stopped smoking marijuana the day before he became a police officer."

The memorandum, written by government investigators, noted that throughout their interview Dowd tried to throw Kenny under the bus implying that Kenny was the leader of their NYPD gang, and Kenny encouraged him to be a participant in criminal activity.

Another problem for Dowd was an interview he gave Mike Wallace for *60 Minutes*, which was broadcast on October 17, 1993. Large portions of the interview were included in the federal government's paperwork.

"I'm not a bum," he told the investigative reporter. "I wasn't a bum before I became a police officer. But becoming a police officer led me in these directions. If your peers happen to be doing these things, then you do them too."

Stunned viewers also heard Dowd explain how he stole cocaine from a murder scene.

**Dowd:** I had to walk past fifteen cops to get it outside into a police car.

**Wallace:** How did you do it?

**Dowd:** I just put the bag over my shoulder, and I walked out the door with it.

**Wallace:** A bag of cocaine?

**Dowd:** Well it didn't say cocaine on the bag.

**Wallace:** And you walked past a line of cops, past the sergeant?

**Dowd:** Well they knew what I was doing. … I know they knew because they were smiling. 'Oh there goes Mike.'

The story was completely different than what he told the DEA.

Dowd added a punchline in the interview.

"Every cop knew what I was doing and what the whole crew of cops were doing in my precinct and in every precinct in Brooklyn."

Career in flames, a criminal case pending, and his family disintegrating like a sand castle built too close to the tide, Dowd wrote letters to the one man he believed would help:

Adam,

Hello, I don't want to say much so I know you understand. No matter what happens to me I hold no ill will toward any of you, just Kenny. Please understand that right now my whole family is in bad shape financially. Anything you could do for me now and in the future would be appreciated. You and I could some day get together for a beer. Know it is set for Nov. 22, 1993 but the government is trying to deny me any credit for what I might have done. So there may be a hearing in a few weeks and sentencing postponed (sorry) ...
Stay strong. I wish your family the best.
— Michael Dowd.

In a second letter to Adam. Dowd suggested he had "an ace or two up his sleeve" and promised to see Adam again, adding, "One day we'll have a beer together in Dominica like we were supposed to."

The Feds said the letters were evidence that Dowd was attempting "to benefit from his criminal associations and seeks for his family still further illicit proceeds from narcotics trafficking."

"No, I believe that he was simply asking compassionate assistance from a former associate," insisted Pavle "Punch" Stanimirovic. "Diaz never ratted out anyone as far as I know. Plus, Adam Diaz is a legend. He was among the best drug dealers in the history of New York. Adam Diaz was the Tony Montana of New York. He and his drug team were getting into the night clubs, living the high life, buying cars and houses, jewelry. His methods, and his connect with Dowd and Eurell was the right thing and the right time. They created the perfect storm of criminals and police working together in perfect lucrative financially rewarding harmony. If you were writing the history of the really great drug dealers—the ones who brought excellent product at decent prices to the people who wanted it—Adam Diaz ranks as one of the most admired and respected drug-dealing gangsters. If they gave medals for outstanding corruption that benefited the local economy and kept the coke quality high, Diaz, Dowd, and Eurell deserve awards."

Federal court documents noted "the cooperation of almost all principal accomplice witnesses, including former officers Kenneth Eurell and Thomas Mascia. Borrent Perez, a/k/a Baron, Adam Diaz, workers of the Diaz organization and the Company."

Diaz turned over the famed "letter to the enemy" note (printed in the *New York Post*) Dowd sent Diaz while in prison which in part stated "I hold no ill will towards any of you, just Kenny."

To interpret that line as encouraging a hit on Kenny would be somewhat of a stretch, although some people are adept at stretching,

The federal case against Michael Dowd didn't escape the notice of New York City Mayor David Dinkins. The depths of corruption within the New York City Police Department stunned even those who thought they knew the score. It was the perfect storm that highlighted the complete failure of the department's Internal Affairs process and the shortcomings of a police department consumed with optics and politics.

At best the Internal Affairs process was anemic. At worst the bumbling detectives inhabiting its offices and field units were eunuchs, castrated by a political commissioner who was more worried about style than substance.

Certainly another element playing into the mix was that impenetrable Blue Wall that separated police officers from the taxpayers that hired them.

Finally there was the money. More money than anyone involved had ever seen. Cocaine users chasing the dragon at the end of a glass pipe spent Lincolns, Hamiltons, and Jacksons as fast as they could get their hands on them—no questions asked. And the things they did to get their hands on those greenbacks were sometimes unspeakable When cocaine was legal in America, there was no link between cocaine and crime.

Michael Dowd knew instinctively that the NYPD's image in the Manhattan media mattered more to the department than what was happening to a bunch of drug dealers, jilted girlfriends, and lowlifes in Brooklyn.

Ultimately NYPD shields gave Dowd and his crew, which included Ken Eurell, a license to steal. And they did. Dinkins, up for reelection in a fierce battle with Rudy Giuliani, appointed former Judge Milton Mollen to head up a commission that would look into the Seven Five and other corrupt precincts that were exposed when Suffolk County made their busts.

The panel was intended to be one of the most high-powered bodies to ever investigate the New York Police Department. Their star witness was Michael Dowd himself. During four televised hours of testimony, Dowd answered questions about his career as a police officer and a drug dealer.

Dowd said he joined the police department to help people but soon realized that wearing blue had ramifications.

"It was us against them out there," he explained to the commission in what would be his only truthful statements on the case. "You the public are not going to beat us the cops, in the streets. We can have our way when we put on the badge."

When Judge Mollen's team issued their report, it identified the problems Dowd exploited and damned the department's failures.

*"What we found is that the problem of police corruption extends far beyond the corrupt cop. It is a multi-faceted problem that has flourished in parts of our City not only because of opportunity and greed, but because of a police culture that exalts loyalty over integrity; because of the silence of honest officers who fear the consequences of ratting on another cop no matter how grave the crime; because of willfully blind supervisors who fear the consequences of a corruption scandal more than corruption itself; because of the demise of the principle of accountability that makes all commanders responsible for fighting corruption in their commands; because of a hostility and alienation between the police and community in certain precincts which breeds an us-versus-them mentality; and because for years the New York City Police Department abandoned its responsibility to insure the integrity of its members.*

*"The abandonment of effective anti-corruption efforts did more than avoid public exposure of corruption, it fueled it. It sent a message throughout the department that integrity was not a high priority and that department bosses did not really want to know about corruption. In short it gave everyone in the department an excuse for doing what was easiest: shutting their eyes to the corruption around them. And that is precisely what happened."*

Mollen, as did every other investigation into NYPD corruption, recommended policies and programs to treat the problem. The commissioners proposed an oversight committee to which the NYPD would be accountable. The committee also suggested a complete overhaul of police department practices including:

- Screening and recruitment
- Integrity training
- Field supervision
- Command accountability

The commission also recommended:

- Zero tolerance for corruption and brutality
- Zero tolerance for drug use by officers
- Better intelligence gathering on the streets

To this day the careers of Kenneth Eurell, now a resident of Florida, and Michael Dowd, who still lives on Long Island, affects the day-to-day activity of every New York City Police officer on the beat and any Internal Affairs investigator who would be looking over their shoulders.

The Dinkins-Giuliani race resulted in Guiliani becoming New York's mayor on January 1, 1994. Giuliani appointed William Bratton as commissioner, and Bratton set about enacting reforms.

"That's bullshit," countered a former NYPD officer who was on the force during the Giuliani years. "Giuliani encouraged corruption, and anyone who says otherwise is full of shit. Any New York cop with an ounce of honesty about dishonesty knows Giuliani's attitude towards corruption, 'Do whatever you can get away with, just don't get caught.' That's no big secret."

"I find it sort of poetic or ironic," commented former New Jersey cop Fred Wolfson who, in the 1980s, provided security for the Reagan White House, "that Ken was sworn in to the NYPD the same month and year that Reagan took office, and this NYPD scandal broke at the same time as the Reagan administration's Iran-Contra Scandal—the most shocking corruption scandal in American history. And in both of these historic scandals, the public wondered just how much the people at the very top really knew about what was going on."

On July 11, 1994, four days after the publication of the Mollen Commission report, Michael Dowd, thirty-five pounds lighter than he had been in his days on the force, appeared before Federal Court Judge Kimba Wood. A onetime Playboy Bunny whom President Bill Clinton wanted to be US Attorney General, Wood listened to Dowd apologize and beg for mercy.

"Thank you. Your Honor, I think the first thing I'd like to do is apologize to each and every police officer that's had to work under the guise I left them two years ago. It's a very difficult job, and I made it much more difficult, and for that I apologize. I also want to apologize to my family. As you can see, they are destroyed.

"My two sons are not present in court today because I didn't think it would be proper to have them here for this. My wife, she is busy with her own life right now. I think I have probably lost her. We will see in a couple of years from now. I apologize to her for this.

"I want to thank ... the Suffolk County Police Department. While it might appear that my life was ruined, it wasn't. They saved my life, and I thank them for that.

"Having a drug addiction and being a police officer is one of the most difficult things there is to deal with. As a police officer, your heart is ripped in half when you are addicted with drugs. There are times I wished I was dead because I couldn't stop what I was doing.

"One day I was driving to work and I was having a heart attack, I thought. Rather than go for help, I pulled off the side of the road so I wouldn't crash and waited for the pains to subside. That night I did cocaine again.

"I lost my job, which I didn't take seriously enough, my family, my freedom. I don't know, Your Honor, what ten or fifteen more years in jail is going to do for me. I know that today I am a different person than I was two years ago, and I am not angry at anybody, and I just would like to be able to live a normal life.

"I thank you. I thank everyone."

Dowd's father also spoke to Wood and said his son was a good man who fell prey to drug addiction.

Wood was not impressed. She told Dowd that he possessed "an immorality so deep that it is rarely encountered. You did not just fall prey to temptation and steal what was in front of you or take kickbacks or sell confidential law-enforcement information," she said.

"You also continually searched for new ways to abuse your position and at times you recruited fellow officers to join in your crimes."

And with that she sentenced Michael Dowd to spend fourteen years in federal prison.

Under his breath, New York's No. 1 corrupt cop whispered.

"Oh my God. Oh my God."

And those years in prison will do what, exactly? Teach him a lesson?

"I'll tell you the lesson," confided a former NYPD officer. "Legislating morality creates criminals. Period. Make beer illegal, and everyone who drinks beer is now a criminal. People don't know, or were never taught, that most illegal drugs in America were legal. LSD was perfectly legal and quality controlled from 1947 to 1965. Ecstasy (MDMA) was legal from 1911 to about 2000. You can't have illegal drugs and safe streets at the same time. Take your pick. In America, politicians choose illegal drugs over safe streets because there is more money in illegal drugs. And corporate prisons where we lock up criminals and that could be you."

Ken Eurell resisted impulses to write to Dowd in prison.

For the first few years I thought of

him often especially since he was in
the federal prison in Florida very close
by. I tried to refocus to rebuilding my
family's life and being the husband and
father I should have been the first time.
I was extremely thankful for my second
chance.

We met again for the first time during
the filming of The Seven Five. We were
filming a scene where we were returning
to the precinct, and they surprised me
by having Dowd standing out front. I
think they were hoping for a dramatic
confrontation, but when we saw each
other we smiled and gave each other a
long hug. You won't see the scene in the
documentary. It was left on the cutting
room floor.

The ongoing relationship of Dowd and Eurell—
fragmented as it is—is one of ongoing redefinition.

Craig Wolff, a writer for The New
Yorker, visited me to do a story in '95
and also visited Dowd in prison. Wolfe
said Dowd told him to pass on to me he no
longer holds animosity towards me. Ha!
Just listen to the Artie Lange podcast
and we know different.

Through an endless barrage of "Fuck you" and "Fuck
you, too" exchanges, these diatribes on Lange's podcast are
punctuated with heartfelt expressions of true brotherly love.
Anyone who knows the vernacular of New York males who
wore guns and carried badges can read between the lines of

exchanges such as this:

"*I still love you, man, but fuck you.*"
"*I love you too, and you can go fuck yourself.*"
"*We just see things differently.*"
"*We **remember** things differently.*"
"*Fuck you.*"
"*Fuck you, too.*"

The good old days weren't all that good, and those days are long gone. Dowd and Eurell are not teamed up in any ventures, but Dowd and Adam Diaz reunited to import and sell fine Dominican cigars named after Mike and Ken's old Precinct, the Seven Five.

The bottom line, and what really matters, is that Mike saved me from eight years in prison, and in return I saved him from a life sentence or death. We would have never gotten away with that outlandish plan. We would have been caught and prosecuted for kidnapping, robbery, and most likely attempted murder. Had he done it on his own, if the Feds didn't lock him up forever, the Columbians would have killed him because they don't leave witnesses behind.

Mike wanted us to be Butch and Sundance, to go out in a blaze of glory. I knew how that movie ended, I wasn't about to let that happen to us. We are both alive today. So is Adam Diaz, Chickie, and most of the other guys. It's time to move on and enjoy the remaining years we have. Maybe not together living the high life, but at peace knowing we survived the events of that time in history.

Adam Diaz made an interesting comment about loyalty and mutual protection. When Mike asked him to go after the guy who shot and killed Transit Officer Venable, he declined because he didn't know Venable personally.

What Diaz essentially said were words such as these: "If I don't know you, it's not my concern. But, if I know you, and we have a relationship, I'm there for you, and I will back you up 100 percent no matter what. That's just the way it is."

Diaz stated a code of honor, an allegiance to a tribal-like loyalty established on the foundation of collective security, no matter what.

The cops have the same code. They are a band of brothers who will back you up 100 percent no matter what. And that's the problem in twenty-five words or less.

Scholar Rich Martin did a study on police ethics and corruption and found that the Blue Wall can cause problems in a police department in much the same way smoking damages a person's lungs. It's a slow and painful death that could have been prevented.

"When this loyalty to the subculture becomes too strong, the solidarity that follows can adversely affect the ethical values of the officers," Martin said in his study titled "Police Corruption: An Analytical Look into Police Ethics." "The typical 'us versus them' mentality creates an allegiance to the members stronger than that to the mission of the department."

Other studies have found that rookie police officers enter their careers looking for fulfilling and meaningful connections. When they are exposed to good cops, those rookies are assets to the force and their communities. The best case scenario for first-year police officers exposed to toxic environments laden with dishonesty and corruption is morale problems. The worst scenario is perpetuation of the corruption and illegal practices.

Beyond the studies of policing, one could argue that when the government makes certain substances illegal, it does not remove the demand. Instead, the state creates crime by pushing the sale and control of these substances into the illegal black markets. All the while, demand remains constant.

We can look at the prohibition of alcohol and the subsequent crime wave. The peak of prohibition, 1930, was the deadliest year for police in American history. Fully 300 police officers were killed and innumerable poor people were slaughtered as the state cracked down on drinkers.

Attempts to legislate morality are doomed. Sweden made coffee illegal in 1746. The government also banned "coffee paraphernalia"—with cops confiscating tea cups and saucers. Once the ban was lifted, Swedes began to consume coffee again and Sweden now has one of the highest per capita rates of coffee consumption in the world.

The point should be obvious: People will continue to use recreational drugs, and cops instructed to enforce laws that are against the proclivities of the population find themselves frustrated, conflicted, and ripe for corruption.

Numerous former drug cops, prosecutors, and judges are members of Law Enforcement Against Prohibition (LEAP). The group, which has recently taken a stance favoring legalization of marijuana, explained its stance in a lengthy statement.

"We believe that drug prohibition is the true cause of much of the social and personal damage that has historically been attributed to drug use. It is prohibition that makes these drugs so valuable—while giving criminals a monopoly over their supply. Driven by the huge profits from this monopoly, criminal gangs bribe and kill each other, law enforcers, and children. Their trade is unregulated and they are, therefore, beyond our control.

"History has shown that drug prohibition reduces neither use nor abuse. After a rapist is arrested, there are fewer rapes. After a drug dealer is arrested, however, neither the supply nor the demand for drugs is seriously changed. The arrest merely creates a job opening for an endless stream of drug entrepreneurs who will take huge risks for the sake of the enormous profits created by prohibition. Prohibition costs taxpayers tens of billions of dollars every year, yet 40 years and some 40 million arrests later, drugs are cheaper, more potent and far more widely used than at the beginning of this futile crusade.

"We believe that by eliminating prohibition of all drugs for adults and establishing appropriate regulation and standards for distribution and use, law enforcement could focus more on crimes of violence, such as rape, aggravated assault, child abuse and murder, making our communities much safer. We believe that sending parents to prison for non-violent personal drug use destroys families. We believe that in a regulated and controlled environment, drugs will be safer for adult use and less accessible to our children. And we believe that by placing drug abuse in the hands of medical professionals instead of the criminal justice system, we will reduce rates of addiction and overdose deaths."

"Drug overdoses are preventable," insists Dr. A. R. Mohammed, one of America's leading experts on drugs and addiction. "The reason we have overdose deaths in the USA is because the people who use these drugs must do it in secret where it is not safe. In countries where they have taken away the criminality and stigma, people don't die of illegal drug overdoses, and you don't have corrupt cops making money off an illegal drug industry because there is no illegal drug industry to corrupt them."

If the reason drugs are illegal is because they are harmful, it would make sense to reduce as much harm as possible. It is proven that the stigma of drug addiction is actually more medically harmful (due to the stress and anxiety it causes) than addiction. If America really cared about young people on drugs, there would be no illegal drugs and no corrupt cops lured into the illegal drug market.

**Question:** In your state, how old do you need to be to buy alcohol?

**Question:** In your state, how old do you need to be to buy cocaine?

Any questions?

# PICTURES

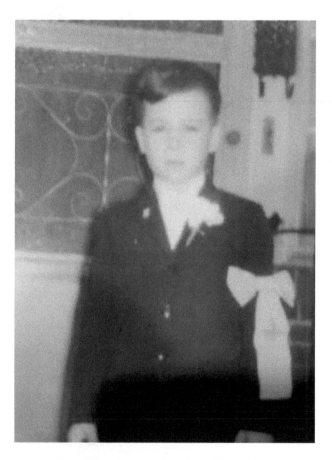

*Ken's First Communion photo (Ken Eurell)*

*A copy of Michael Dowd's NYPD identification
card. (Author's collection)*

*Ken and Dori Eurell and their children in happier times (Ken Eurell)*

*Ken and Dori just after they started dating (Ken Eurell)*

*Ken Eurell and his partner Frank Essig celebrate after earning overtime paychecks. (Ken Eurell)*

*(l-r) Michael Dowd, Walter Yurkiw and Ken Eurell at movie premiere. (Ken Eurell)*

*NYPD photo of Michael Dowd. (Author's collection)*

*Ken's corvette and new house, bought with cocaine money. (Ken Eurell)*

# BIBLIOGRAPHY

*NYPD: A City and Its Police*
By James Lardner, Thomas Reppetto
Henry Holt and Company, New York, 2001

*Chief!*
By Albert A. Seedman and Peter Hellman
Arthur Fields Books, Inc., New York, 1974

*New York Confidential!*
By Jack Lait and Lee Mortimer
Crown Publishers, Inc., New York, 1951

*USA Confidential*
By Jack Lait and Lee Mortimer
Crown Publishers, Inc., New York, 1952

*Prince of the City: The True Story of a Cop Who Knew Too Much*
By Robert Daley
Warner Books, New York, 2005

*Buddy Boys: When Good Cops Turn Bad* (Kindle Edition)
By Mike McAlary
Open Road Integrated Media, 2015

*Dancing with the Devil: Confessions of an Undercover Agent*
By Louis Diaz and Neal Hirschfeld
Gallery Books, New York, 2010

*Good Cop Bad Cop: Detective Joe Trimboli's Heroic Pursuit of NYPD officer Michael Dowd*
By Mike McAlary
Pocket Books, 1994

Joey Diaz video podcast "Mike Dowd Two Night Special Event, Night One"
https://www.youtube.com/watch?v=iyI-DFne8YY

Joe Rogan Experience "#707—Michael Dowd"
https://www.youtube.com/watch?v=TVt2CJewjFE

Artie Lang Podcast "Artie officiates on-air fight between two crooked cops"
http://soundcloud.com/artie-lange-podcast/artie-officiates-on-air-fight-between-two-crooked-cops

# ACKNOWLEDGEMENTS

The authors wish to thank Henry Guevara, Baron Perez, Adam Diaz, and Pavle Stanimirovic for consenting to interviews for this book and for any photographs they may have contributed.

The existence of the Mollen Report on .pdf was an invaluable resource. The report is available on the internet at: *https://web.archive.org/web/20110721230958/http:// www.parc.info/client_files/Special%20Reports/4%20-%20 Mollen%20Commission%20-%20NYPD.pdf*

Frank C. Girardot, Jr. would like to thank J. Brian Charles for providing insight into his father's experience as a construction worker in Brooklyn during the 1970s and 1980s and for allowing early promotion of the book online at http://www.thehill.com.

Girardot especially thanks Sarah Favot for her patience, important insight, and moral support as the early drafts of this book were being crafted.

Burl Barer gives special thanks to Barbara Chait Creme for her patience in putting up with his odd writing hours to complete the manuscript on time, and to everyone at WildBlue Press involved in the book's publication and promotion.

Barer also thanks Howard Lapides, Magic Matt Alan, and Mark Boyer of *True Crime Uncensored* on Outlaw Radio USA for allowing my continual blatant self-promotion.

Follow the authors on Twitter:

@KenEurell

@FrankGirardot

@BurlBarer

Use this link to sign up for advance notice of the next book from Burl Barer and Frank C. Girardot, Jr:
http://wildbluepress.com/AdvanceNotice

Word-of-mouth is critical to an author's long-term success. If you appreciated this book please leave a review on the Amazon sales page:
http://wbp.bz/biba

**Available Now From WildBlue Press:**
**FAILURE OF JUSTICE**
**by JOHN FERAK**

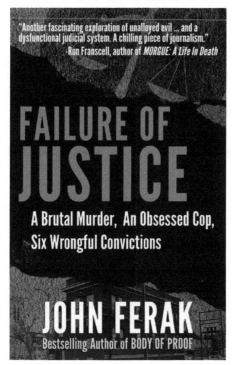

Read More: **http://wbp.bz/foj**

# FAILURE OF JUSTICE

## 'MAKING A MURDERER' TIMES SIX!

If the dubious efforts of law enforcement that led to the case behind MAKING A MURDERER made you cringe, your skin will crawl at the injustice portrayed in FAILURE OF JUSTICE: A Brutal Murder, An Obsessed Cop, Six Wrongful Convictions. Award-winning journalist and bestselling author John Ferak pursued the story of the Beatrice 6 who were wrongfully accused of the brutal, ritualistic rape and murder of an elderly widow in Beatrice, Nebraska, and then railroaded by law enforcement into prison for a crime they did not commit. FAILURE OF JUSTICE is the story of the crime, the flawed investigation and rush to judgment, as well as one man's refusal to accept an unjust fate, and the incredible effort it took to make the state admit it was wrong.

Check out the book at: **http://wbp.bz/foj**

**New From WildBlue Press:**
**THE POLITICS OF MURDER**
**by MARGO NASH**

Read More: **http://wbp.bz/pom**

# THE POLITICS OF MURDER

*"A chilling story about corruption, political power and a stacked judicial system in Massachusetts."*–John Ferak, bestselling author of FAILURE OF JUSTICE.

On a hot night in July 1995, Janet Downing, a 42-year-old mother of four, was brutally stabbed 98 times in her home in Somerville, a city two miles northwest of Boston. Within hours, a suspect was identified: 15-year-old Eddie O'Brien, the best friend of one of Janet's sons.

But why Eddie? He had no prior history of criminal behavior. He was not mentally ill. He had neither motive nor opportunity to commit the crime. Others had both. Yet none of that mattered because powers far beyond his Somerville neighborhood decided that Eddie needed to be guilty.

As laid out in THE POLITICS OF MURDER: The Power And Ambition Behind "The Altar Boy Murder Case", the timing of this case did not bode well for Eddie. A movement hoping to stop the supposed rise of young "superpredators" was sweeping the nation, and juvenile offenders were the targets. Both the Massachusetts governor and an elected district attorney who personally litigated this case supported juvenile justice reform, and both aspired to higher offices.

Eddie O'Brien's case garnered both local and national publicity: He was the youthful Irish Catholic boy next door. His grandfather was the retired chief of the Somerville Police Department. Court TV covered the trial in adult court gavel to gavel, calling it the altar boy murder case. His highly publicized case changed the juvenile laws in Massachusetts. Other states began to follow suit. But did the justice system fail Eddie?

Check out the book at: **http://wbp.bz/pom**

**More True Crime You'll Love
From WildBlue Press.**

Learn more at: http://wbp.bz/tc

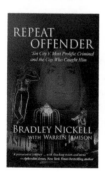

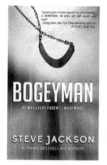